Comes To The Light
Learning About the Entangled Families of Edgefield, South Carolina

Donya Papoose Williams

Copyright © 2017 Donya Williams

All rights reserved. No part of this publication may be reproduced, distributed, or transmitted in any form or by any means, including photocopying, recording, or other electronic or mechanical methods, without the prior written permission of the author, except in the case of brief quotations embodied in critical reviews and certain other noncommercial uses permitted by copyright law.

Published by Donya Williams
www.comestothelightlat.wixsite.com/comestothelight
www.genealogyadventures.vpweb.com

Printed and Bound by Createspace

ISBN-10: 1975649958
ISBN-13: 978-1975649951

First Edition

First Printing

Nonfiction Disclaimer:
The advice and strategies found within may not be suitable for every situation. This work is sold with the understanding that the author is not held responsible for the results accrued from the advice in this book.

Cover Design: Donya Williams
Editor/Publicist: Brian Sheffey

DEDICATED TO THE ANCESTORS OF
EDGEFIELD, SOUTH CAROLINA

"Frameless"

I am a compilation of all who were before me; a puzzle without a frame and many missing pieces: An assigned 'label,' but not necessarily my name. Our searches may seem futile; frustrating for sure, but worth every moment. Our ancestor's strength in desperate, inhumane situations; their determination and refusal to be erased, are why we're here. Seeds planted in alien and hostile soil-, brought forth generations of unlimited hope, despite impossible odds. Seek and speak their names. Learn and teach; sing the songs of lineages-, even if only in part. Our future depends on the stability of the present and the present-, good or bad-, is undeniably an outgrowth of the past. I am honored to honor my genetic 'framers.' (Soon as I find them.)

Figure 1 - *Poem and Photo Submitted by S. Alexander*

Table of Contents

Acknowledgments .... **vii**

Chapter 1 – Edgefield, South Carolina **1**

Chapter 2 – The Spiritual Connection **5**

Chapter 3 – The Oral History of The Yeldell Family **12**

Chapter 4 – Focusing on Annie Mae **37**

Chapter 5 – Researching my Mother's Paternal Great-Grandmother ... **42**

Chapter 6 – Ezra Adams And Liberty Springs Baptist Church **74**

Chapter 7 – The Petersons **86**

Chapter 8 – The Senior Family **102**

Chapter 9 – Moses Williams **108**

Chapter 10 – A Confusing Mix-up **118**

Chapter 11 – John Yeldell a.k.a Rev. Elijah F. Flemon **125**

Chapter 12 – The True Accounts of the Rev. Elijah F. Flemon **165**

Chapter 13 – Calling All Branches **170**

Chapter 14 – Honoring the Ancestors **176**

Acknowledgments

First, I want to thank my Lord and Savior, Jesus Christ. The challenges I faced were big, but for you they were small, and I am forever grateful to you for allowing me to learn about my family which in turn taught me a lot about me.

To **Aunt Lula (R.I.P)** and the entire Robertson/Yeldell family. It was the size of her family and the information she gave me that started me in the direction that led to this book, but it was the closeness of her descendants that kept me going. You guys are the inspiration for bringing our family back together. From the bottom of my heart, I thank you.

To my mommy, **Juanita Yeldell-Williams** and my sister **Tamara Yeldell**, thank you for your encouragement and your support in keeping me focused. I love you dearly. To **Alexis, Marcus, Demetrius,** and **Cameron**, you are the reason I pray that God allows me to see another day. Because of you, I will always strive to be the best. Mommy loves you.

To **Uncle Brother (R.I.P),** who was the first to refer to me as the family historian. I know that his spirit, along with others, continues to guide me. To **Uncle J. Carlton** you were the first to start this journey. It took me almost 25 years to get to your ending point. Thank you for telling me what to look for. I hope that I am making you proud.

To my cousins, **Brian Sheffey** and **Sheila Hightower Allen** you two have been my rocks. Without the two of you and the rest of my researching family your support, guidance and fact-checking, this book simply would not be.

Finally, to all the ancestors; because of you, we are here. Thank you for your persistence and your push for us to reunite. For too long your descendants have been separated. You are slowly bringing us back together. For that, I thank you.

Figure 2 – *Town of Edgefield Entrance, taken by Julian Hunter Pendarvis, 15 July 2017*

Chapter 1 – Edgefield, South Carolina

Before there was a North and South Carolina there was just the Carolinas and the two together were considered a province or a territory outside of its main country. The main country was Europe and Charleston was the main hub of government for the entire area. The province of the Carolinas was founded in 1629 by eight Lord Proprietors. These eight men were George Monck, Edward Hyde, John Berkeley, William Craven, Sir George Carteret, Sir William Berkeley, Sir John Colleton and Anthony Ashley Cooper. They were awarded this land by Charles II of England for being his biggest supporters in winning back the throne that his father had before him.

A Lord Proprietor is a fancy word for a landlord and it was through these men the Carolinas were populated. They populated the area through a system whereby they granted one hundred and fifty acres of land to each member of a family[1] as well as offered religious freedom. Every religious belief was welcomed, except for atheism. Slave owners who owned twenty slaves or more also known as Planters were promised one hundred and fifty acres of land per slave. This incentive along with the religious toleration, political representation in an assembly that had power over public taxes, and protection from Spanish attacks drew 6,600 settlers to the colony. These incentives attracted English Settlers, French Protestants (Huguenots) and other colonists from Barbados and the West Indies.[2]

The northern side of the Carolina province was settled by the people of Virginia who were considered the poorer group, while the southern side was settled by the Aristocrats – the ones with the money. The Aristocrats came from places like Barbados where the business of slavery was very well established. It was through that establishment that over 40% of African Americans traveled to Charleston to be placed into the Carolina slave trade. The southern part of the Carolinas became the leading place for slave trading in America.

The Carolinas began to grow in different directions and a call for a formal separation came into play. The separation started in 1710 by splitting the southern part of the Carolinas into four counties, Berkeley, Colleton, Craven, and Granville. This split helped for a little while, but the differences, politically speaking, between the two areas continued to push them further apart, and by 1729 North Carolina and South Carolina was created. Over the course of about forty years, South Carolina kept the four counties they originally started with until 1769.

In 1769, all four counties were disbanded and formed into seven new districts. Those districts were: **The Ninety-Six District, Beaufort District, Camden District, Charleston District, Cheraw District, Georgetown District** and **Orangeburg District.** The Districts were created as a political move towards individual governing and created judicial seats in each county. The northern sections of the old counties of Colleton, Granville, and Berkeley made up the Ninety-Six District. In almost thirty years the Ninety-Six District was abolished and six smaller counties were created in 1785. Those counties were **Abbeville, Edgefield, Laurens, Newberry, Spartanburg,** and **Union.** As growth continued in 1798 other cities were formed. Below are the areas that were formed from the six counties that were originally formed in 1785:

- Abbeville Co. (Formed 1785)
- Part of Abbeville Co. to Greenwood Co. (Formed 1897)
- Part of Abbeville Co. to McCormick Co. (Formed 1916)
- Edgefield Co. (Formed 1785)
- Part of Edgefield to Aiken Co. (Formed 1871)
- Part of Edgefield to Greenwood Co. (Formed 1897)
- Part of Edgefield to Saluda Co. (Formed 1896)
- Laurens Co. (Formed 1785)
- Newberry Co. (Formed 1785)
- Spartanburg Co. (Formed 1785)
- Part of Spartanburg. Co. to Cherokee Co. (Formed 1897)
- Union Co. (Formed 1798)
- Part of Union. Co. to Cherokee Co. (Formed 1897)
- The Ninety-Six District from 1785 to 1798 consisted of present-day Union Co.

It is the Ninety-Six District that our families began to build what we know today as Edgefield, South Carolina. The men who ruled this part of South Carolina did so with impunity and without question. It was a political powerhouse that was very instrumental in the forming of what we know as America today. There were thirty-one battles fought in South Carolina during the American Revolution and most of the men who fought came from the Edgefield area.

They were soldiers who shaped the character and the history of the county and fighting for what you wanted was not frightening to them, it was mandatory. It was that fight that exists and grew in all Edgefieldians. For those who continue to research the area recognizes that the same fight, they began to learn about within their ancestors is the same fight that exists in the descendants today. The men and women who started Edgefield county were the epitomai of pride, honor, and assurance.

To this day there are large numbers of family members who still live in Edgefield. Before I started my research, I didn't know any of them. But now my research has introduced me to over 200 surnames all attached to my family. My research has put me in touch with my history in a way history classes and textbooks couldn't have come close to doing. The American history that I have learned, along with the family history I've discovered is visceral. It's unvarnished. It's an intrinsic part of who I am. It shaped my ancestors who, in turn, shaped me. The history of Edgefield is the history of my people, be they white, black, Native American or a mixture of all three. My research has put together a family tree for the history books and as you read on you will see why.

Figure 3 – *Springfield Baptist of Edgefield Cemetery,*
Photo taken by Donya Williams

Chapter 2 – The Spiritual Connection

I was born in New Jersey in 1972. My mother moved back to the Washington, DC area with my daddy and older siblings in 1977 when I was five years old. By 1984 we moved yet again to Virginia Beach where I believe the most important part of my childhood was spent. It was in Virginia Beach that genealogy first introduced itself to me. To jump straight into what finally caught my interest would have me talk about my first experience of my family "haunting me" as a teenager, but if I started from that point, the story would become confusing. I find it best that I start at the beginning of my journey into the researching of my family by giving a small background into who they were starting with my mother.

My mother was the baby of fourteen children, 8 girls, and 6 boys. Juanita was born in Washington, DC in 1939 to Jefferson and Annie Mae Senior Yeldell. As an adult, she was the only daughter who moved around and over time, she would come to live in Bishopville, South Carolina, Paterson, New Jersey, Virginia Beach, Virginia and Jacksonville, Florida. The first five years of my life were spent around my father's family in New Jersey, but by 1978 my parents had come back to Washington, DC, were separated and I was no longer connected to my father's side of the family.

In 1984, my mother moved to Virginia Beach and apart from one of her brothers and a few of my cousins from her side, who would visit us in Virginia Beach, my family never had the opportunity to know me nor I them. When mom came back home to Washington, DC for good in March of 1990, I was back around her family again. However, by mid-August of that same year, I was off to college, leaving me yet again with very little time to get to know my mother's family. I was born at a disadvantage of not knowing anything about my mother's family because my grandparents, an aunt, and an uncle died before I was born. This disadvantage, in terms of opportunities to hear about my Yeldell history, made me an easy choice for genealogy.

I was chosen by genealogy at a very young age. It was a selection or calling, that I fought off for many years. I fought researching off because it seemed ghostly, even spiritual in some ways. I have always been afraid of the unexplained and at one point in my life; my biggest fears were ghosts, weird noises or things that went bump in the night. However, everyone has had a moment in their life when there was no explanation for an unusual occurrence happening to them. Whether it was a picture falling off the wall or an object not being in a spot that you know you placed it previously; these unexplained occurrences happened to me on a regular enough basis for me to begin to take note. I am not saying that I believe in the supernatural, however, I do think my ancestors haunt their loved ones. Not haunt as in to frighten, but haunt in a manner that lets you know they are there, and that you are not alone. It was through those fears, however, that genealogy had started to make its choice.

My first experience happened when I was thirteen years old. It is a common thing in my mother's house to do a big cleaning on the weekends, and this weekend would be no different. My sister and I would start it out by going into my mother's room and talking with her before we started. There didn't have to necessarily be a reason to go in her room, we just did. I would go and get in the bed with her and my sister would either stand at the door or sit in one of the chairs in her room while we had these morning talks.

On this particular morning, she didn't seem to be herself. She kept looking around as if she had lost something. She said to us, "Y'all, I think my sister was here." As I said before, she was the only girl in her family who had moved around. Her sisters hadn't ever visited her previously, so what was she talking about? What made matters worse was the sibling she was speaking of was deceased, so how could she have been here? I knew that she had to be speaking spiritually. Because I was scared back then of that kind of thing, I immediately jumped out of her bed and with a tone of voice like Arnold's from "Different Strokes" I looked at her and said, "What you talkin' about Mommy?"

She smiled and said, "I felt her all throughout the night. I asked her to leave me a sign that she was here and to let me know that I wasn't dreaming but I can't find it." By this time my sister and I just looked at my mother. I thought she was going crazy. But then she looked up and said, "There it is." My sister and I looked up and on the ceiling, was a handprint. Not just any handprint but we believed it to be my Aunt Margaret's handprint. She had long bony fingers and just as clear as day this handprint, that appeared on the freshly painted ceiling had long bony fingers. I, of course, ran out of my mother's room and didn't go back in there for about a month.

Almost fifteen years later, my Aunt Margaret visited again. This time she didn't come to see my mom. She came to visit me and my family. It was 1996, and I was back home from college and was pregnant with my second child. While I was watching the TV my then two-and-half-year-old daughter was playing in the corner by the window. I realized she was laughing and talking with someone so I looked over to her and said, "Alexis, who are you talking to?" She responded, "I am talking to this lady, she is really funny." With me still being afraid of the unexplained I sat up as quickly as a pregnant woman who felt and looked like she was carrying quadruplets could, and asked, "What lady!?"

My daughter laughed at me and told me she was talking with

the lady by the window. I was confused because there was no lady by the window, and I proceeded to get up off the bed to prepare myself to get me and my daughter out of there. Something within me made me ask, "Alex, what is the lady's name?" Alexis turned to the window and said, "My mommy said what is your name?" And just as quickly as she asked the question my daughter turned to me with an answer and said, "She said her name is Margaret." I looked at Alexis and said, "Well, you need to tell Margaret to go home." She laughed and said, "Mommy, she said you are silly." Without any hesitation, we left my house for four hours and went to my sister's. While there I called my mother, who was now living in Florida and told her to come and get her family.

I didn't realize it then, but those early encounters were preparing me for what I deal with today and what I see as genealogy making its choice. I am a firm believer in GOD and believe that he allows things to happen and to guide you in the way he wants you to go. GOD's direction for me seemed to be genealogy and I didn't know it then, but I was being chosen through those unexplained events. Unfortunately, I was so afraid of those types of occurrences that I wasn't heeding that call and another route had to be taken.

How Genealogy Pulled Me In

A few months after my experience with my Aunt Margaret, my mother was back home and her sister, Lula, was celebrating her 80th birthday. There were five generations of women living in Aunt Lula's family line and she and her girls took a family picture. Aunt Lula was the fifth child of Jefferson and Annie Mae, but the second oldest girl. She was the first female in our family since her maternal grandmother and namesake, Mama Lula, to live to the age of 80. Aunt Lula was feisty and an excellent cook. She baked delicious rolls, but her specialty, in my opinion, was her cakes.

Figure 4 – Lula Yeldell Robertson, Photo courtesy of Jennell Yeldell Turner

Aunt Lula's family is the largest and represents the bulk of Jeff and Annie's descendants. I thought it was amazing to have five generations in a family alive at the same time. So, I asked my mom if she knew exactly how many children, grandchildren, great-grandchildren, and even great-great-grandchildren her sister had. My mom was not sure, but she did try to count for herself her sister's children. It was easy to count the children because they grew up with my mom, all of them being so close in age.

What I mean by that is because my mom was the last-born child of fourteen, some of her sisters had children before she was even born. This meant she had nieces and nephews who were either older than her or very near her age. It began to get difficult, however, when she got to the grandchildren, the task of counting them became more of a challenge. The challenge was impossible once she got to her sister's great-grandchildren. She suggested that I call Aunt Lula and ask her. This was something that I didn't want to do alone, so we called her together. Mommy spoke with her first, using sister talk to break the ice. She then finally told Aunt Lula that I was on the line and that I wanted to ask her a question.

I said, "hello Auntie" and then asked, "Aunt Lula, how many children do you have?" Aunt Lula, being who she is, said, "What you get Juanita to call for? I am not going to bite." I told her "mommy wanted to know too (with a slight grin in my voice)!" Yes, I lied to my Aunt but I didn't know what else to say. She responded in the classic Aunt Lula style "[in] deed, I don't know." At that point, my mom and her sister began to count nine children, twenty-four grandchildren, forty-two great-grandchildren and four great-great-grandchildren living during that year. As my mom and Aunt called out those names I was in awe because those names began to flow like water would flow over a waterfall, my mouth dropped to the floor.

When they finished, I said, "Wow, Auntie, you have almost one hundred people in our family all by yourself!" To have that many people in one family, and knowing that these two sisters came from their own large family of fourteen siblings, thirteen of whom had children, I was fascinated. I started to wonder about the size of the entire family. I didn't know this then, but this was how genealogy was pulling me in, not with those who had passed on, but with those living right here and now.

I still had not given in to the call, but learning this information did spark my interest in the size of my family. Life went on and some years had passed and, just like all families, my family continued to grow larger every day. But what was amazing about my family's growth was how it would happen. It was a normal thing to have at least three Yeldell women pregnant at the same time, so if this happened at least twice during a year the minimum number of children added to my family annually was six (not including multiple births). Realizing how fast my family grew started me thinking again about how big my family is.

I decided to call my mother to discuss the family. Instead of limiting our count to her sister Lula's children, we were going to count all of her sibling's children. We created a list that included my mommy, her siblings, and their children. In other words, we counted all of the descendants of Jeff and Annie Mae Yeldell. I typed into an Excel spreadsheet while she recited the names of her mom, dad, and all of her siblings. I placed my grandparents at the top with their children's names, listed from the oldest to the youngest. Beneath each one of her siblings, we added the names of their children under them, and so on.

Where we didn't know the names but knew relatives existed, we substituted the words "unknown name". We wrote down every family member we could think of from my grandparents down to their 4th, and possibly 5th, great-grandchildren. This process went on for almost hours. When the spreadsheet was completed, it revealed that my grandparents, Jefferson and Annie, had 330 living descendants. There were so many names we knew and just as many names we didn't know. Looking at all of those unknowns, I wanted to know who my grandparents' descendants were.

I wanted to know them as people rather than just names in a spreadsheet. I used that spreadsheet as a starting point and sent sections of the spreadsheet to key people in my aunts' and uncles' families so they could fill in the names of those unknown relatives. As this happened, not only did I have names to replace the "unknown" slots, the list became larger. My final count was very close to 500 family members. There were so many relatives I knew about but had never met. It seemed only natural to start planning family reunions.

We had two reunions: one in 2008, and the other in 2010. Although they both turned out to be nice events, they did not receive the necessary support to move forward. Neither the 2008 nor the 2010 reunion have more than 100 family members in attendance. However, because of those reunions and the information that was collected on the spreadsheet, I didn't want to stop. I wanted to know more about my family. Now that I knew the names of my grandparents' and their descendants, it was only natural to learn about my ancestors.

*Figure 5 - Jefferson and Annie Mae Yeldell,
Photo taken by Addison Scurlock Photography*

Chapter 3 – The Oral History of The Yeldell Family

Like most families, the Yeldell's were very proud people. They knew that their grandparents had been instrumental in the early building of communities of color in the Washington, DC area and, that their uncles had made great strides in local and national government, but what was it that we didn't know. These were all things to be proud of, however, something within me thought that there was something more and I wanted to know it. The only way that I could begin to find the answers to the questions that I had was through Genealogy. I started with the stories or oral histories I had heard.

My grandparents were born in the mid to late 1890s. Now, I don't know about some folks, but to me, that was a long time ago and they were pretty old. Jefferson and Annie Mae Senior Yeldell migrated out of South Carolina during the Great Negro Migration[3]. Oral history says that both Jefferson and Annie Mae were born and raised in a place called Edgefield County, South Carolina. I was told that my grandmother was born in the city of Edgefield in January 1898, while my grandfather was born in neighboring

Greenwood in June 1894. Although they were said to have been born in two different places, one in a county the other in a city, the two were close enough for them to meet and court one another.

The proximity of their neighborhoods allowed them to work together, go to the same church, and probably go to the same school, that is if they even went to school. I don't know what age they were when they met, or how long they courted, but in December 1913 Jefferson (age 19) and Annie Mae (age 14) were joined together in marriage. When they married, grandma was pregnant with their oldest son, Lt. Col. Thomas Jefferson Yeldell. Thomas was born in May 1914. Every eighteen months, from 1914 through 1923, they had a total of six children born in Edgefield, South Carolina. Their names were: Thomas, John Carlton, Edward (Uncle Buddy), Ida Mae (Aunt Sis), Lula and Jeannell.

Oral history taught me that in 1926 my grandfather spent a year on the road. What my family didn't know was during that year there were two separate addresses in two different states. This was not because they had separated, but more so due to jobs becoming harder and harder to find during the Jim Crow era and rising racial tensions in Edgefield. One address was in Asheville, North Carolina and the other was in Richmond, Virginia. Research shows that the two addresses were listed in my grandfather's name and that his occupation was a laborer in both places.

Despite the traveling back and forth between homes, in June 1926 they had their seventh child Davis Lee Yeldell in Asheville, North Carolina. Around 1928 they moved to Washington, DC. Between 1928 to 1939 they had seven more children roughly eighteen months apart yet again. This time producing: Robert, Margaret, Joseph (Uncle Brother), Evelyn, Josephine and her twin sister who was stillborn and never legally given a name, and finally my mother, Juanita.

Coming out of the south, to finally settle in the District of Columbia, proved to be an excellent move for them. Like New York, DC was in the prime of its own version of the Harlem Renaissance and my family was right in the middle of it. It was in DC, where they began to build a legacy. This legacy wasn't just for their children. They built a family legacy for generations to come. They were both spiritually grounded people who seemed to have had an anointing over them. Some intangible thing which enabled them and their family to go out into the world and accomplish great things regardless of the circumstances. It was because of that anointing they followed in their family's footsteps and built upon a foundation that was created within them by earlier generations.

We always knew about one church that our grandparents were founders of a few years after they arrived in DC, but we didn't know that they were the founders of two churches in DC. Springfield Baptist Church located at 508 P Street, NW, and Greater New Hope Baptist Church now located in downtown DC. It was the founding of these churches that my grandparents began their own personal legacy. I learned that my grandparents had attended Southern Baptist Church when they first moved to the DC area. As my research went on I learned that several of the families of Edgefield who moved to DC attended this church as well.

There was a falling out between my grandfather and one of the top men at Southern Baptist, which led him to leave. When they left, several other families left as well. It was with those families that they were co-founders of a church named New Hope Baptist Mission. New Hope Baptist Mission was organized on November 23, 1933, at the home of Chester L. Smallwood. The devotional service was attended by George Tyler, Jesse Drumming, James Simmons, Yeldell, and Smallwood, who was also the moderator. They all spoke on the subject of creating the church and agreed that the church would be formed under the above-mentioned name. I found that under the list of founding members of the New Hope Baptist Mission (now known as Greater New Hope Baptist Church) not only were my grandparents listed, but their two oldest sons were also a part of the founding of this church. However, something happened and they ended up leaving this church too.

It was at this time Jefferson and Annie Mae founded Springfield Baptist Church. Oral history taught us that Springfield Missionary Baptist Church of Washington DC was named after the church the two of them met and married when they lived in

Edgefield, South Carolina. It was founded in November 1939, the year my mother was born. According to the original members of Springfield Baptist Church of DC, my grandparents were the top financial backers of the church... and much more.

At the inception of Springfield, just like with New Hope, I learned they were at the devotional meeting that formed Springfield. My grandfather was the Chairman of both the Trustee and Deacon Board and President of the Senior Choir. His presence was well-known throughout the church. All would call on Jeff when there was a problem. My grandmother was just as visible as my grandfather. She was the Chairwoman of the Deaconess Board, and Founder and President of the Women's Auxiliary Club, the Pastor's Aid club, the Nursing Unit, and the kitchen committee. She ensured the children of the church received the spiritual background they needed in their life as well as receiving what they needed for school and holidays.

My grandparents touched upon every aspect of this church. Through my research, I found deeds and public records that would back up my findings. Both churches still exist today. I thought this achievement was a pretty cool thing for a man with a 6th-grade education and a woman with a 4th-grade education. It was incredible that two people with a grade school level of education could achieve something like this. Little did I know at that stage in my research that they were far from the first in their family to achieve something on this scale with such a limited educational background.

The youngest Yeldell of my family to attend Greater New Hope Baptist was my uncle Joseph. He would have still been a baby. With me researching my family after my older aunts and uncles had passed to the memory of founding, let alone attending this church was lost. Springfield was the last church my grandparents, aunts, uncles, and mother attended and it was the only church the next generation of Yeldells knew about. My mom and her siblings attended Springfield Baptist with their parents. As they grew older and had children of their own, some of them attended Springfield as well.

Springfield was originally a traditional looking, castle-like church, rich with a historical background that carried memories strong enough to, in my opinion, give anyone a certain type of feeling just by looking at it. You know that feeling when you'd walk past a building and you would just

Figure 6 - *Springfield Baptist of DC, Photo taken by Charles Cooke*

look at it and know something happened in there. I continued to research and eventually proved that feeling to be right. In its hayday, it was host to well-known preachers and singers.

It was the first recording site of the world-renowned gospel singer, the late Madame Edna Gallmon Cooke. Another well-known gospel great singer was Sister Wynonna Carr, who was also no stranger to Springfield either. The nationally known Rev. C. L. Franklin never came to DC without attending service in Springfield and his daughter Aretha Franklin would sing along with my mother in the children's choir. My mom once told me that Aretha asked her to be a part of the group she was forming, but when she asked my grandfather if she could do it, he told her no. I was right, the founding of these two churches placed the Yeldell name in Washington, DC history.

My grandparents rubbed elbows with the upper echelon of African American families during their lives in DC. They were friends with Justice Thurgood Marshall when he was a lawyer, and their personal photographer was the now nationally-known and recognized black photographer Addison Scurlock. Due to the times, they lived in and the people they knew, the status and respect of the Yeldell name spilled over to their children.

Since they lived in an era where men were lifted more than women, that status allowed the boys to prosper and grow into highly respected and recognizable individuals. They became educators, high ranking military officers, and locally and nationally known public officials. This is not to downplay the role of the girls and the women within the family. They were the epitome of that old saying 'behind every good man there is a better woman'.

The boys could not, and would not, have been who they were without the aid of their mother and sisters. The Yeldell name became well-known in the Washington, DC area. Along with that notoriety came a celebrity type status. That status may not have been a national or as glorified as that of actors or musicians, yet even today one can't mention the name Yeldell in the Washington, DC area, especially to residents who were native to DC for the last 50 years, and not have the name recognized. I do not carry Yeldell as my last name, but whenever anyone has learned I am a Yeldell, they expect great things from me just because of who my family is.

The building Springfield was in became old and the congregation outgrew the space. The picture shown below is a picture of the old and newer Springfield. The new Springfield was built right next door approximately thirty-years later. The original Springfield was eventually turned into a daycare center. I can remember attending the newer brown church as a little girl. I used to be afraid of it because it was the stereotypical black church with shouting and great singing. However, when there wasn't a service going on, it was also a safe haven for the children of 6th street and its surrounding area. The activities they provided kept the children out of trouble while providing what I see now as self-esteem building exercises for those who came from troubled homes or who just needed that extra support.

For example, they had a summer league boys' basketball team with cheerleaders that played against other churches and recreational centers. This wasn't just something to do either both the basketball and the cheerleading teams competed in tournaments that required travel. One of my fondest memories of Springfield was being one of the cheerleaders and traveling to Pittsburgh for a game and competition. Springfield provided something to do every single day, whether it was offering space for kid projects or planning trips to nearby amusement parks for the entire family to attend. Springfield provided a type of support to families as a whole which I believe was a serious glue to holding the black families together.

When I became an adult, I ended up working there as the first communication assistant. My job was to create newsletters and flyers, as well as overseeing all of its social media sites. I never had a reason to go into the original Springfield church building until I needed to get information about the daycare center. As I entered the building, I was immediately overwhelmed with a strange feeling. It wasn't a bad feeling, but it was the kind that produced visible goosebumps on my arms. I was talking with the Director and she saw an expression on my face that made her ask if I was okay.

I explained, "I've never been in this building, but, now that I'm here I'm getting this strange feeling."

She asked, "You are related to the man whose name is on the building, aren't you?"

I responded, "Yes."

She said, "It is him."

She proceeded to tell me stories of parents who would walk into the building and have a good feeling while being inside the church. I smiled at what she was saying and was mesmerized, and perhaps even overwhelmed, by the feeling I was receiving at that moment. I told her that it might have been the spirit of my grandmother. She always took care of the children of the church. The director saw the peace and happiness on my face and said, "It is good to know they are watching over us." It was weird to me because experiences like that use to run me away but this time it pushed me towards finding my family.

Starting the Search for Jefferson Yeldell

I was new to genealogical research and thought it best to start slow. In my mind, this meant researching one grandparent at a time. My grandmother, Annie Mae Senior, died at an early age. Nevertheless, my mom and her siblings seem to have known a lot about her and the **Senior** family. They didn't, however, know anything about

Figure 7 - Jefferson Davis Yeldell, Photo taken by Addison Scurlock Photography

their father's **Yeldell** family. It made sense to me to begin my research with him.

Before I started my search, I needed to understand what I was about to get into. I had to prepare my mind for what I was going to find. To do that I had to remember the period he was born in. So, I thought back to what I learned in school and mixed it with the oral history I was taught at home. I had to prepare myself for everything I might find as an African American. The possibility of finding slaves, the much talked about rapes of female ancestors, and even incest-driven relationships, due to the separation of family members over the course of generations, might be revealed.

To understand Jefferson Yeldell and his family, I had to learn about, and understand, Edgefield itself. What was it like geographically? What was it like culturally? And what was it like historically? What were the day-to-do norms of Edgefield society? I told myself that no matter what I found I would be open to it all. Taking that knowledge into perspective, my journey began.

With the Yeldell name being so rare, I didn't think it would be too hard to find the information that I needed. This was another reason I began my search with him. Since Ancestry.com says all you need is a name that is exactly what I used. When I typed in my grandfather's name on Ancestry, I found him as an adult in the 1920s, living in South Carolina, and again in the 1930s, living in Washington, DC. In both U.S. Federal censuses, he was listed as married with children. The 1920 census showed him living next door to a man named Gary Yeldell, who was younger than him. There was no sign of Jefferson, however as a child. Since I didn't know the name of his parents, nor anything about his siblings, I had no idea who Gary was. I thought about another way to find Jefferson and decided to cold call and email people with the last name Yeldell.

I went through phone directories and email listings, contacting anybody with that last name. I was hoping they would know something about their family that could possibly have a connection to my family. Maybe even find a descendant of the man Gary who lived next door to him. While I made these random calls and sent out several emails to strangers, I learned that Yeldells, regardless of their nationality, either didn't know much about their history or didn't want to share it. I would get responses from those I contacted with stories that began with, "My father told me this white man was my granddaddy, but I never knew how" or "I think my family was a part of the Underground Railroad because my family was so secretive."

There was one story, however, that stood out to me. I sent an email to a white Yeldell and received a response. He said that he didn't know much about his dad, but that he would connect me with his mother. I explained to her who I was and what I was doing. His mom and I talked for a little while. She told me that because she had married into the family, she didn't know much, but what she did know she would share. Because genealogy research was new to me, the obvious questions I should have asked, like her husband's parents' name, I didn't ask. What she did say was revealing. She said her husband was very secretive. That wasn't shocking because my grandfather had been secretive too. I had no idea of it at the time, but, I would come to learn that secrets were what made Edgefield County what it was.

However, the story this kind lady was sharing with me became very interesting because as she started to describe the type of man her husband was I felt like she was talking about the men in my family. She described him as a medium to tall man with skin that was of olive complexion. He was extremely intelligent and a true lady's man. She said he was kind and gentle and protective and that he always treated her like a queen. Her description was amazing. Apart from the skin color, he could have been any Yeldell man I knew. I thought that was awesome, but I realized this was going to be a slower process than I thought. Finding my grandfather's family would not be easy. Instead of giving up I switched my strategy and decided to talk with the oldest relative in my family, Aunt Lula. At this point, she was my mother's oldest living sibling.

When I asked her about her daddy's side of the family, she ended up being a dead end as well for the simple fact that she wasn't certain of the basic information a genealogist requires, including the names of Jefferson's parents'. Her exact words were,

"I think their names were Peter and Katie." I think! How do you not know your grandparent's names? At that moment, I decided to switch to my grandmother because the search for granddaddy was proving to be too difficult. But as the search went on for her I found there was no luck there either. The reason why was pretty straightforward: the only times I had seen Annie Mae in official records was also the first and only times I had found my grandfather. I was at a standstill.

I came upon several disappointments and dead ends while searching the census records online. Finally, I took a trip to the National Archives in Washington, DC and learned individual census records were sealed for 72 years. This delay in making the census records publicly accessible prevents people from viewing information during a person's lifetime. This was good to learn. However, it should not have stopped me from finding my grandfather or grandmother, as children. I didn't know what to think or even what to do. I had become so discouraged that eventually, my motivation started to wane and I would stop my research for periods of time. My search became very intermittent. I would only continue my search if something came up until, finally, I very nearly stopped altogether. Although I had not stopped completely, I began to let things block my search, like the death of family members.

My Aunt Lula, who was one of my first partners in genealogy, and my Aunt Evelyn had died along with several cousins, and a favorite uncle. I loved my family and it hurt me when they died. Yet, I don't think anything hurt as much as losing my uncle, Robert Lee Yeldell, who died 6 January 2007. He followed my development from childhood and played an influential role in my life. From my participation in gymnastics to my schooling through college, he knew more about me than any of my other aunts and uncles. Once I returned home from college, he made sure that we caught up on each other's lives. He

Figure 8 - Robert Lee Yeldell Photo courtesy of Juanita Yeldell-Williams

was the kind of uncle who made every niece and nephew that knew him feel like they were his favorite. The good-natured battle over who his favorite niece or nephew is, continues to this day. In a very real way, he was the closest I came to have a grandparent.

As special as he made his family feel, he was even better for the residents of Washington, DC. He served on several committees in the southeast area Washington including The Advisory Neighborhood Committee (ANC) and The Mayor's Service Area Committee for Ward 8. He was one of the Founding Members and two-time Vice President of the Ward 8 Democrats. His service went even further into the building he lived in. Uncle Rob volunteered for the Senior Citizen's Counseling, the delivery service for Park Southern Apartments, and served as President of the Park Southern Resident Council in 1990, and was also the President of the Park Southern Neighborhood Co-op in 1995. He held both positions until he died. During his funeral Councilmen Mendelson vowed to set up some type of scholarship in his name but like politicians do I think that it was just talk.

What I do know is that Uncle Rob was loved by many people and was the epitome of why my family so amazing. After the funeral, representatives of the building where he lived told us during a private repast, "To honor your uncle we want to change the name of the building and name it after him." So, what used to be called Park Southern Apartments in Washington, DC is now called Robert L. Yeldell Tower – a Park Southern Community. The family was surprised. We had been calling it Yeldell Towers for many years because several family members lived in the building at the same time. On 7th July 2007, the name was changed officially and we were all there to see them unveil the new awning.

Figure 9 - Yeldell Towers, Photo taken by Donya Williams

I realized with the change of the name of a building, other changes would have to happen, such as phone book entries, local maps and what is said and viewed when public transportation stops in front of the building. When riding the buses in the Washington,

DC area the name of your stop is displayed and a recording calls out the name of that stop. Because my uncle was so special to me, changing the public transportation information was my way of honoring him. Since my family history research was at a complete standstill, I turned my attention towards DC Metrobus to change what is reflected when the bus stops. On 29 June 2010, I saw it. While riding the bus, I was playing a game on my iPod and suddenly something in my mind said, "Donya, look up" and there it was in bold and bright lettering: **YELDELL TOWERS**. The people on the bus probably thought I was crazy when I started talking to myself out loud. I stopped the game I had been playing and frantically fumbled to get my camera. I missed taking the picture that day, but I did call my mother, my cousin Robin (Uncle Rob's daughter) and my sister, Tammy, and told them that when you ride bus numbers D12, D13, D14, W15, W19, A6 and A46 to or from the Southern Avenue station in southeast Washington, the Yeldell name appears and his full name would be announced.

Now I am sure you are wondering what does this have to do with your research? Not long after I saw the sign on the bus the research that was once at a standstill suddenly picked up. I went from a period of having no information to finally discovering clues. It was as if honoring my Uncle Rob began the turnaround for me and my research. I decided to look for my grandfather again and when I did I looked through the same records I had previously viewed while visiting the National Archives online. This time, I located my grandfather as a boy.

I found not just my grandfather, but his parents and his siblings on the 1900 U.S. Census, where my grandfather was five years old. His parents were Peter and Katie, and his siblings were Martha, Eddie, and Gary! I realized that Gary was the same name of the man that had lived next door to him in the 1920s. The reason I found neither him nor Gary before became clear, their first names had been spelled differently: Granddaddy wasn't listed as Jefferson in the 1900 Census, he was known as Jeff. Gary's name had been spelled as Gairy.

The same problem happened with my grandmother, but with a slight twist. The photo below shows her family listed in the 1900

Census as John Señior, Lula Señior, Lula Señior (the older daughter, age 3) and Lula Señior (the youngest daughter, age 5 months). For my grandmother, the first mistake was the fault of the census taker. It was as though he didn't care what he wrote when taking the information. For whatever reason, he had repeated the name of my great-grandmother for her two daughters. What made things worse was how the last name was transcribed. I am guessing that this record was transcribed electronically.

If you notice in the snapshot below[4], the letter "n" in their name is written with the Spanish letter "ñ". If the transcription was done through an automated electronic scanning machine rather than by human hand, then the Spanish letter "ñ" was converted

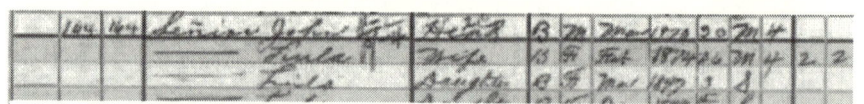

Figure 10 - *Snapshot of 1900 U.S. Federal Census, Snapshot taken by Donya Williams courtesy of NARA*

turning their last name into "SeÃ£Â±Ior". It was no wonder that I couldn't find them online through Ancestry.com or at the Archives. Next, I looked at the birth dates for the two girls, which were March 1897 and December 1899. Respectively both dates were within a year of my grandmother's. This left me unable to determine which one was actually her. Regardless of the slight hiccup with my grandmother, the information I found was wonderful. It was as if God had opened the floodgates and allowed my ancestors to teach me and guide me in the direction necessary to learn all that I could.

Ancestry.com has a feature for members to leave messages asking questions about their family in general, or specific ancestors. These are called Message Boards. These boards allowed other researchers to share or learn more information about their family. They give you the opportunity to talk with those who may have sensitive information that for some is not easy to talk about like slavery. Learning who enslaved your family can be a tough pill to swallow and the same feeling can be had by the descendant of those who have learned that their family actually owned someone.

The message board provides a platform to have those types of conversations. We know that Africans were kidnapped and brought to America as enslaved people, they lost everything, their culture, their religion and their birth names. Being owned by a family made them the property of those who enslaved them. Once freed through the 1862 Emancipation Proclamation, this made them have to start over. Some of the newly freed African-descended men and women assumed the surname of their owners, while others took the surnames of the enslaving families they knew were theirs through blood kinship.

At this stage in my research, I didn't know if my Yeldell ancestors took their surname through some non-genetic bond with their Yeldell enslavers – or whether they had a blood right to the name. It was because of these message boards I met a direct descendant of the Yeldell family on the Yeldell family message board. Candace Wellman is a direct descendant, and 4th great-granddaughter, of William and Mary **Steifel** Yeldell. She left messages in my Ancestry.com message inbox, giving names and other information for her 4x great-grandparents. She also disclosed that her family had indeed held enslaved people in Edgefield. This was an exciting find.

When I first spoke with Candace, who lives in Washington State, she had been conducting research on the Yeldell name for over 20 years. She was my first teacher of genealogy and remains a great resource for me to this day. Because of Candace, I was learning what to look for when researching my Yeldell family in Edgefield, as well as how to look for it. On 11 September 2010, the Yeldell's of Washington, DC met the Yeldell's of Washington State. Candace, her son, Jimmy, and another cousin named Judy, who is also a descendant of William and Mary Yeldell, traveled to Suitland, Maryland to meet my family.

We met in the dining hall of the building my mother resides in and had an informal 'bring your own dish' type of setting. We ate, laughed, shared what we knew about our personal family history, listened, but more importantly, learned. I assumed Candace 4th great-grandparents were my family simply because they shared the last same last name and the pictures of the Yeldell farm she gave me were very valuable. I was looking at photos of where my mother's paternal family may have lived, as well as other ancestors in our family.

One of the biggest mistakes in researching is to never assume. Assuming in researching terms means the other person is always right. You must search and find the information for yourself. Candace taught me that because of the rareness of our last name, all Yeldells, regardless of their nationality, come from one common immigrant named Anthony, a Quaker shoemaker who came from the Merstham Parish in Surrey County, England. Learning this from Candace made me want to find evidence of this for myself, and push even further to find more facts. I am so glad I did because there really was so much more to learn.

Putting Things in Order

Meeting Candace, and taking in what I had learned from her, I realized my work had been very scattered when I first began to research my family. For example, when I first started my search, it had initially been to learn more about my grandfather, but when I couldn't find him I switched my focus to finding my grandmother. I needed to keep some type of order. Returning to my research, I understood I needed to be more focused and targeting. I returned to researching Jefferson Yeldell. However, if any, records should surface regarding my grandmother, Annie Mae Senior, I would limit myself to saving them, keeping them for the time when I would come to focus my research on her.

With a new focus, I found my grandfather in all of the available census records during his lifetime. I found my grandfather as Jeff, aged five, along with his parents and three siblings in the 1900 U.S. Census. I then found him in the 1910 U.S. Census, aged seventeen, where he still lived with his parents and siblings. I rounded his life out with the 1920, 1930 and, finally, the 1940 census. Between the 1920 and 1930 census, I found addresses my grandfather had once lived through city directories. These are records on Ancestry.com that document where a person lived. They were the first version of the white pages. The earlier versions of the white pages focused more on the adults of the house and in most cases, gave the occupation of the head of the house.

In all three areas that he lived my grandfather was listed as a laborer. The more I researched, the more attention I paid for things I normally would not have noticed. After organizing my thoughts, I had accomplished my first goal of finding my grandfather. I realized that I had revealed the human version of what the writers of the hit Disney movie "The Lion King" called the circle of life. Just like that movie. I was watching my grandfather grow from a child into an adult, and then into a man. He was a man who kept the Yeldell family circle going through his children.

Before I started researching, I knew my grandfather by name only but now I was in the position to tell his children information they didn't know. I could tell them the names of their aunts and uncles. I could confidently say to them that granddaddy lived next door to his brother Gary in the 1920s and that their four older siblings, although for a short period knew or met his mother and other siblings. I could say to them that in 1926-27, granddaddy lived at 1711 Venable in Richmond, Virginia, while Annie Mae and the children lived at 90 Mountain Street in Asheville, North Carolina. However, the most important thing I could tell them was that their father was not born in Greenwood but in Edgefield just like their mother. I know you are thinking, wait not born in Greenwood? But Donya you said at the beginning of the book that your grandfather was from Greenwood, South Carolina and that your grandmother was from Edgefield how and why did this change?

As South Carolina grew like any state new cities would emerge and because my grandparents were born so far back the possibility of towns being created after their birth was great. My family didn't know that at one-point Greenwood and Edgefield were one in the same. But as I stated in Chapter one, Greenwood was founded in 1897, three years after he was born. I also realized that everywhere granddaddy and his family lived was in Edgefield, not Greenwood. So, where did my family get the oral story about him being born in Greenwood? According to my mother, her father told her. I did learn, however, when the postal lines changed one could be living in Greenwood in one year, and then the lines would change again and you would now live in Edgefield. Where he lived changed constantly possibly without even knowing.

Finding Jeff's Family

I was confident with my search and proud of the new-found information that I could share. I started to feel as if I knew exactly what I was doing. In other words, my researched moved on from being the hit-or-miss affair to a continuous find or clue. I was no longer like those who have newly engaged with genealogy and family history research. The research of my grandfather and his family was difficult, but every now and then something about him and his family would just drop in my lap. I learned that my grandfather sibling's names were Edward, Martha, Gary, and Janie (she was found in the 1910 census record). Now that I found my grandfather, I was going to try and find the descendants of his siblings.

You would think that Gary would have been the easiest since he lived next door. But just like his brother, he and his children were just as difficult to find. Gary's son Henry was the baby that was living next door with his mother and father in 1920. What happened to Henry's parents, Gary and Mary? I finally found Gary's oldest son Henry through the Social Security Death Index. This is a database that was created in 1962 and was a record of all those whose death was reported to Social Security. Henry had died in 1970. But, where was Henry after 1920 but before 1970?

I continued my search for granddaddy Jeff's brother Gary. I was finally able to find Gary by finding his death certificate. Gary's life was short lived. He was born in 1897 and died at the age of twenty-eight in 1925. So, the 1920 Census would be the last one he would be included in. However, before his death, Gary had registered for WWI by completing a draft card. On the card was information about where he lived and that he had a wife and son that he would be leaving behind if drafted. He and his wife Mary also had three more children before his death. I found Gary's death certificate in a database called South Carolina Death Records.

This database was a compilation of death records dating from 1821 to 1965. This provided a lot of information as well about Gary. It told me the date of his death, how he died, who his parents were, the last place he lived before death, what he died from and where he was buried. The information that you receive from a death certificate is extremely important, but it is only as good as the person who is providing it. There is a space on the death certificate where the person who is providing the information can sign called the informant signature. It is typical for the informant to be a family member, which can be another research avenue in terms of identifying members of the extended family for the individual you are researching. If this person doesn't know the parents' names or any of the other information that I was given about Gary then that information was left blank on the certificate making that death certificate useless.

I was fortunate that Ancestry.com had the South Carolina Death Records as one of the databases accessible to their members. It was there that I found not only Gary's but several other family members', death certificates. With each relative's name I found, I learned of additional ancestors. As I searched through this database, I ended up finding Gary's daughter Anna Jane Yeldell. Anna was Gary's second oldest child who died as a baby. Her death certificate cited Gary and his wife Mary as Anna Jane's parents.

This record also listed the cemetery she was buried in which was Bailey Bethel Church in Greenwood. In this instance, the informant was my granddaddy, Anna lived to be four months and 29 days old. Her cause of death was reported as perforated malarial fever. Gary went on to have two more children with Mary, Robert, and Kate. He would pass in 1925 when he succumbed to chronic heart disease. I wanted to continue my research on Gary and find his grandchildren in the hopes that my mom could meet more of her family.

As I stated earlier, I found information for his oldest son Henry in the U.S. Social Security Death Index. This does not give as much information as the actual death certificate, but it provided a listing of information that included the person's name and social security number, the last known address, the date the person was born and the date the person died. Henry was born in 1920 and died in 1970. Henry's U.S. Social Security Death Index and a census record were the only records I had pertaining to Henry. Searching for him in additional census records was turning into a search just as frustrating as my initial search for my granddaddy, Jefferson Yeldell.

However, the more I researched Henry Yeldell the better I became at online record searches. I knew that when viewing the census records you don't just look at the family you are directly researching. You also look at the families living around the family you are researching as well. This is done because the families living around could very well be an aunt, uncle or in my grandfather's case a brother. We know that Henry's father, Gary died in 1925 so he would not be listed in the 1930 census record. So, I began to focus more on Henry's mother.

Looking at his mother, Mary, I learned that she had remarried after my Uncle Gary had died. Mary married a man named John **Harrison** Sr. and had five children by him. When I found Mary, she was living with her husband and children from both marriages. However, in the 1930 census, her son Henry did not live with her. As I viewed the rest of the census record, I found Henry was living just two houses away with his grandparents, John Henry and Hester **Gaskins Palmore**.

I knew this was him because the age was right, and he appeared to have been named after his mother's father. Finding this explained why I couldn't find Gary's other children. They no longer used the Yeldell name. Gary's other son and daughter were now listed as Harrisons. Once this was found, I was able to find everything I needed for all of Uncle Gary's children. I wasn't able to get my mother to meet her uncle Gary's children because they had all passed on but she did speak to his son Robert's only daughter, Barbara, his widow Helen **Dansby** Yeldell and his son's niece Delphine Dansby who ended up living not far from where my mother lives now.

There was far more to this story. I didn't know it yet, but finding Mary was just the beginning of finding out that we were a very entangled family. This meant I had an additional surname to add to my research: Harrison. I now had five Edgefield-connected surnames to research: Yeldell, Senior, Palmore, Dansby, and now Harrison. Little did I know these five names didn't even scratch the surface when it came to my family's history in Edgefield. At this stage, I assumed my genealogy would be the kind of traditional, genealogy that was shown on television genealogy shows, or in books on the subject: a series of distinct, unrelated family lines converging with the union of two people. Perhaps it was the for the best that I was completely unaware of what I would eventually find in my research.

I had found Gary and his children which made me feel really good about my research. I tried to find my grandfather's older brother Edward but there was some confusion that I couldn't get through mixing him with another man with the same name and birth year. His sister Janie seemed to have disappeared too, not able to be found after 1910. So, I started to work on his sister Martha. I did my due diligence and began calling around. This time I called the church my grandparents were married in and spoke with the secretary sister, Dorothy Ryans.

I explained to her who I was and what I was doing. I explained that I had some questions about the record keeping for burials at the church. This was important because it would allow me to not only know who was buried at the church but also where they were buried. She directed me to the church groundskeeper, Ulysses Freeman, and gave me his telephone number. I thanked her for the help and called him later that day.

When Ulysses (pronounced Yoo-Lis-see) answered the phone, I explained to him that I was researching my family and that I wanted to know if he knew exactly where my grandparents were buried. During the conversation, we talked about them (somehow without mentioning their names) and their parents, and, in doing so, I mentioned my grandmother's mother, Mama Lula **Peterson** Senior. Mentioning her name worked out well because he knew who she was immediately. He even explained to me that he didn't live far from where her house used to stand. He went on to say that although it is old and no one has lived there for years the house was still standing. It was a great conversation.

Returning to the original reason why I called, Ulysses shared that the past church records pertaining to burials were not very well kept. It was at that point he asked me what my grandparent's names were. I told him their names were Jefferson and Annie Mae Yeldell. When I said that there was a slight pause, then he said in a surprised tone, "Jeff Yeldell! My daddy had an uncle named Jeff Yeldell." This time an awkward pause happened, and then I responded, "Well, who are your daddy's parents?" Ulysses responded, "Nathaniel and Mattie Freeman." I was speechless! My grandfather had a sister named Martha, and Mattie could have been a nickname for Martha. Could I be talking to my grandfather's sister's grandson?

The conversation became more in-depth as he shared with me that his grandmother had ten children and that their names were Willie and William (who were twins) Peter, Katie Lou, Cleveland (Ulysses's father), Oscar, Andrew, Sampson, Anna, and Robert Lee. He called out one name that my mother knew was her cousin, Kate Lou. We learned that Kate Lou had stayed with my mother's parents for a little while in DC when my mother was a little girl. It was at that point we confirmed that Ulysses was the grandson of my grandfather's oldest sister Martha.

I eventually found Martha's death certificate. Her death certificate had both Peter and Katie listed as her parents. According to Ulysses, all of his aunts and uncles had passed. His grandmother, Martha had died in 1933 of Influenza. It was beautiful to find a first cousin once removed from my mother's family, especially since she was the youngest and never had the chance to really meet her extended family when she had been a little girl. The **Freeman** family was yet another new surname I added to my list.

The Missing Sibling

The story of Gary's wife Mary **Palmore** Yeldell directed me to my grandmother's Senior side of the family. I wanted to keep things in order, so I tabled the story of Mary until I started the research of my grandmother making sure it was not mixed with the research of my grandfather's siblings. To recap, I had found Jefferson Yeldell's older sister Martha, her children, and his younger brother Gary, and Gary's children. Martha and Gary's children connected my family to yet more surnames.

My grandfather's younger sister Janie, his brother Edward, and his father all disappeared after the 1910 census. I checked the South Carolina Death Record and U.S Social Security index, and could not find them in these records. There was no sign of them anywhere. It was at this point that I learned that before 1 January 1915, having a death certificate in South Carolina was not mandatory; especially for black people. It was also incredibly rare for a black person to have an obituary in a local or regional newspaper. So, if for example, Peter died before 1915, and if there was no family Bible that recorded his death, he died without legal documentation. I was unable to find anything about Peter. I did, however, discover that his wife Katie died in 1919. On her death certificate, she was listed as a widow at the time of her death.

She had died of something called dropsy. I found that Dropsy was a condition we now know as congestive heart failure. If the information was accurate on the death certificate this would mean that Peter more than likely died after the 1910 census, which was the last record of him being alive but, before 1915 when death records for African Americans were not mandatory. I thought about this and wondered why did he just disappear. At that moment, an eerie feeling came upon me, one that I knew I wasn't ready for. I started to wonder since he lived in the Deep South, could he have been a victim of a lynching? Why did this thought jump on me like this? I wasn't ready to face that question and just walked away.

Running from the thought of my great-grandfather being lynched, I looked at the records of my grandfather again, reviewing all of the census records that I saw him on making sure that I didn't miss or bypass anything. I discovered that in 1900 my great-grandparents, Peter and Katie, were married for seventeen years, had eight children, of which only five lived. In 1910, they had been married for twenty-seven years, had ten children, with only six who survived. I noticed that in each census I would see one less child than the number cited in the preceding census record.

This meant there was another child, an older child, who was not listed by name on the census. His or her existence was simply supported by the total number of children Peter and Katie stated they had had in the census records. I didn't understand why I didn't know who this person was. I realized this child had to have been older than Martha. Martha was still cited on the 1900 census, while the child missing wasn't. I went to check the 1890 U.S. Census and it was unavailable.

I hit my first proverbial brick wall. All genealogists/family historians encounter this problem sooner or later. I wasn't prepared to have my brick wall moment quite so soon. The 1890 U.S. Census was destroyed or damaged by smoke, water, and fire on 10 January 1921. Anyone conducting research on their family born during 1880 would not see them until the 1900 U.S. Census. There was one more thing that I noticed in the U.S. Census records. Every 10 years the information requested by the census would change. For example, the 1900 and 1910 U.S. Censuses asked how many of the mother's children were born, how many of them lived, and the length of time the parents were married. All census records after that didn't ask those questions. I was lost and didn't know what to do. I also realized I wasn't as skilled as I thought, so I walked away from this problem and decided to come back to it later.

Later, for me, was a few years down the road. That was the time when I started to work with several new genealogists, all of whom were my family. This group had helped me and taught me so much. It was because of them that my researching skills had graduated to DNA and genetic genealogy. What is DNA? DNA, or deoxyribonucleic acid, is the hereditary material in humans and almost all other organisms. Genetic Genealogy is using the DNA to discover new relatives and the common ancestor between you and that newly found family member. My mother was the first person whose DNA I had tested. She had agreed to take a DNA test through a company called 23andMe in February 2012.

The way you take the test is simple. The company mails a kit that contains a test tube with some fluid in it. She would spit into a tube that already had liquid in it. This liquid preserves the DNA sample. The tube is marked by a line and you have to spit in the tube until the saliva and liquid mixed together to reach the line. Once you do that, you close it up, and then shake the tube, and then mail it to the testing company. The results are sent to you via email in six to eight weeks. I had forgotten about my grandfather, Jefferson Yeldell's missing sibling until my mom's results came back.

When my mother's results came back, there was definitive proof that Ulysses was her cousin. We knew this because he had done a DNA test with the same company and showed up as a genetic cousin match to my mom. He was labeled as a 1st to 2nd cousin or close relative. She matched a few other people that I had found throughout the years as well. However, there was another cousin listed for my mother whose DNA match was confusing. She was a female, and her match to my mother was listed as a 1st to 2nd cousin or close relative just like Ulysses.

The only problem was my mom had no idea who she was. A match like that could only mean that someone in her family line was my mother's first cousin. So of course, I sent her a message. I had developed a pretty standard inquiry message for newly discovered DNA cousins over the years. I would say "Hi, my name is Donya Williams and I am the granddaughter of Jefferson and Annie Mae Yeldell." From there I would let them know that I would love to talk and see how we were related. Some would respond while others would not. She was one of the DNA matches who responded.

Her name was Evelyn and she had no idea who the Yeldells were. Evelyn worked with me and my cousin, Charles, who was also working on the Yeldell line. Charles was handling the line through Ulysses, and Evelyn ended up matching both he and my mother extremely high. We didn't know how we were related until Evelyn had found news that was personal to her. At that point, she said that she would handle things herself, but would keep us in the loop. We let her know that we were here if she needed us, and let her handle it from there. She would give us updates every now and then.

Then one day she had figured it out. Her father was the grandson of a woman named Anna Jones. Anna was Jefferson Yeldell's sister. The find was amazing! In the beginning, we hadn't known if Jefferson's unknown and missing sibling was a male or a female. Evelyn had figured it out. It was an awesome find and explained where Gary and Mary got the name of the daughter who passed as a baby. It was also just about all that could be done at that time when it came to researching my grandfather's immediate family.

I could not believe what the search had revealed. I started my search on my mother's paternal line with one surname, Yeldell, and had ended up with six more names and those names were: Dansby, Freeman, Harrisons, Jones, Palmore, and Senior. Armed with those names, I added even more surnames through their children's marriages and their descendants. Finding four of the six children my great-grandparents had, they had over 35 grandchildren and hundreds of great-grandchildren. All of this from two people. What had I gotten myself into? I started to reflect on what I'd learned and focused on it so that I could get started on the search for my grandmother.

Figure 11 - Annie Mae Senior-Yeldell, Photo taken by Addison Scurlock Photography

Chapter 4 – Focusing on Annie Mae

I typed this question in Google search: Can a deceased relative become a person's, Guardian Angel? It generated over ten pages filled with possible answers. The answer I liked most was from a website called angeltherapy.com. This website is managed by Doreen Virtue, a spiritual doctor of psychology and a fourth-generation metaphysician, known around the world for her connection with the realm of the angels. It said:

> *"Guardian angels are sometimes confused with "spirit guides." A spirit guide is a loving being who has lived upon the earth in human form. Most spirit guides are deceased loved ones, such as grandparents, siblings, beloved friends, and parents."* [5]

If this is true, then I think that my spirit guide is my grandmother, Annie Mae Senior-Yeldell. Why? Because I always wanted my grandparents around, specifically my grandmother, and I believe she was the one who stayed around me. I can remember a story when I was sitting in the kitchen of my cousin Cynthia's house talking with her and her friend. As we discussed family, her friend realized how much I accepted the fact that my family was always around me and she asked, "who were the two ladies standing behind me?" I am sure you are thinking 'what two ladies, you only mentioned three people in the kitchen?' I will keep her name secret because we don't want people thinking she was crazy, but Cynthia's friend was a Seer.

A Seer is a person who has a connection to the spiritual realm, and the two ladies, she was speaking of were from the spiritual realm. I told her that one of them would certainly be my grandmother. I didn't know who the other lady could be. I showed her pictures so that she could perhaps try to identify them. Without telling her who my grandmother was, she pointed to a picture of her. She said the other was my cousin Camille's mother. I was glad to know that I was right about Annie Mae and that she is always around. I felt a love for her as if she was right here. There was no doubt in my mind that from the pictures I saw she was the most beautiful woman in the world.

There were several times during the research of my grandfather, Jefferson when my grandmother's side would jump in. As I stated earlier, I wouldn't ignore the information that I found, but would instead put it to the side. However, the more I put the information to the side, the more my grandmother's family would intervene. It was almost as if the Senior family was trying to tell me to start looking for them. Since I already had some research information for her, I started to add her side of the family to my family tree. Conducting research on her and her family was the best way for me to get to know her.

The biggest part of researching is talking with your elder family members. There is always a story they can tell you to start you off in the direction you need to go. So many of my aunts and uncles had passed that, by the time I started to concentrate on my grandmother's family, my options of learning about my grandmother's line were slim. I had to go to my mother who was probably too young to really know anything. Nevertheless, she told me what she could.

My mother could remember spending summers with her mother in Edgefield at her maternal grandmother's house. My mother was a very dainty little girl, who didn't run, and certainly never played rough. She told me a story of how she had a cousin, Gennie B., who was close to her in age. Gennie couldn't run and play due to illness. The two of them would sit on the steps of their grandmother's house and play with their dolls. My grandmother's parents were sharecroppers who grew everything from cotton to vegetables to fruit. She told me how she could remember her mother's siblings, her mother's parents, and the house they all lived in. She said the land that the house was on stretched as far as the eye could see. My mother was also able to share with me some family names that she knew were related to my search.

The problem was she didn't know how those names connected to one another, much less how they connected to the Senior family. It's the same for just about any family. Children grow up hearing names like 'cousin Joe' or 'Aunt Susie' and accept these people as such. How these people were related wasn't necessarily explained. In other words, the context of how they were related to the family was missing. So, I took those stories and started my search for Annie Mae and her family.

Annie Mae Senior Yeldell was born 9 January 1898 to Johnnie **Senior**, Jr. and Lula **Peterson** Senior. She was thought to have been the fourth born of seven children. As I stated earlier, the first time I found my grandmother was the first time I found my grandfather, which was in the 1920 Census. Once I learned how to research to find more information about them, I found what I believed to be my grandmother, her parents, and another little girl in the 1900 U.S. Federal Census Records. Both girls had the same name as their mother. Although each girl's birthday was within a year of my grandmother's, I didn't have enough information to confirm which little girl was her.

However, I knew that was her and her family. I went on to find them again in the 1910 U.S. Federal Census. This time, her first name was there but the last name was still wrong. Annie was listed as Anna M Simos, aged 12 years old, born about 1898, and she had an older sister. Since the baby in the 1900 census was born around December 1899, and the older child in 1897, I guessed that Annie Mae had been the baby referenced in the 1900 Census. Her sister Mollie (I later learned her full name was Margaret Senior) had been the oldest daughter.

I noticed that each census record had them listed as mulatto. When most people see or hear the word mulatto they instantly think that the person has one African American parent and one Caucasian parent. To be honest, a mulatto is a person with parents, and ancestry, of two or more different races. This could mean a white mother and an Asian father, or a Native American mother and an African American father. Oral history taught me that my grandmother's family was my Native American side because of my great-grandfather, Annie Mae's father, Papa Johnnie Senior. Annie's father was said to have been a full-blooded Cherokee Indian. This may have been the reason they were listed in that way.

There were four new Senior family siblings in the 1910 U.S. Federal Census. Their names were: Letha, Charlie, Jennie, and Essie. I shared my findings with my mother and she said, "Yes that sounds about right. Wait, Charlie, who is that?" My mother didn't know about Charlie because by the time she started visiting Edgefield he had moved to McDowell, West Virginia. She was either too young to remember him or, once he left Edgefield, he had never come back and had lost contact with his family. During that time period, children did not get involved in grown folks' conversation.

Even if he was discussed amongst the family, my mother wouldn't have known because she wasn't listening to the conversation of adults, or at least wasn't supposed to have been listening. This made it very easy to not know who he even was. Charlie was among the first group of unknown ancestors I would introduce to my mother on her mother's side of the family. As I continued to research my grandmother I found even more of her siblings. Their names were: Hollie, John, and Moses Lewis (M.L. for short). My mother knew about the last two but didn't know about Hollie.

Hollie was another one of my grandmother's younger brothers. However, the way I found Hollie was not through the census, but through the South Carolina Death Records. I saw that Hollie's parents were Lula and Johnnie Senior on his death record. He had died of Typhoid Fever at the age of twelve. My mother had never heard of him, nor that her mother had a sibling who had died at such a young age. These new discoveries meant that instead of my grandmother being one of seven children, she was, in fact, one of nine.

I had gone full circle with my grandmother fairly quickly. Apart from the spelling of the Senior name on one census, it was easy to do. I had already found my grandmother as a baby in the 1900 census and, as an adult, with her husband on the 1920, 1930 and 1940 U.S. Federal Censuses. I also found that she had lived in previously unknown towns, thanks to three different U.S. City Directories. Now that I had found Annie, it was time to research her siblings and prove some of the family's oral stories, just like I had done Jeff. But for some reason, I couldn't do this with her. I did know that more surnames needed to be added to the fray. Her sister Mollie married a **Chinn** while her sisters, Essie (1st m **Kemp**, 2nd m. **Ryans**) and Jennie married twice (1st m. **Peterson**, 2nd m. **Addison**). Her brother Charlie had added the name **Fisher** to the mix.

Chapter 5 – Researching my Mother's Paternal Great-Grandmother

Researching Annie Mae Senior's siblings were pushing me into discovering more about my great grandparents – and identifying my great-great-grandparents. Every time I wrote down a name, a birth date, or a death date, it led me into this earlier generation of the family. I realized that sometimes the direction that you want to go with genealogy isn't always the way that you should go at that time. I wanted to know more so instead of forcing the hand of my grandmother's siblings, I gave in to the great and great-great-grandparents. Besides, my grandmother's siblings were opening up a story that was too soon for me to talk about at this stage of the book and my great and great-great-grandparents were guiding me in my search now, so they were leading the way.

Researching had allowed a spiritual door to open and my ancestors had gone through it and closed the door behind them. I realized there were stories that needed to be told. Acting as gatekeepers, they would choose which family story would be revealed, and when it would be revealed. Now that I had their help, everything that needed to come out, in terms of my family's history, would begin to do so. My ancestors were making themselves known to me. They showed me that I was not as afraid of the unexplained anymore and that I was starting to accept the feeling and the nudges that I was receiving. This was a good thing. I jumped right in and learned about the first census taken.

The first nationwide census was taken in 1790 and every ten years after that. Free people of color were counted in this census, but as living with a guardian or a person who was taking care of them like a mother takes care of her child. However, if an African American was enslaved, and not free, then they were not included in the census. Now don't get me wrong, they were counted, but with the inventory that included the animals or any other property, the owners may have had. The first census to count enslaved African Americans separate from the inventory was called a slave schedule. There were two. The first Slave Schedule was done in 1850 and the second in 1860.

These schedules were created because the north wanted to have some way of tracking how many times an enslaved person would change owners. However, the south felt that if you placed their names on these schedules then it would make them human, something slave owners felt they were not. A compromise was made and by not adding their names, but giving their ages, they were not counted as people, but as property. They were listed on these Schedules with just the age, sex, nationality, and gender of each enslaved person. This census also allowed southerners to up the number of representatives in Congress. I am sure you've heard of African Americans being three-fifths of a man. Well, this is where that came from. So now instead of being counted directly with the inventory it was its own separate list.

The 1870 Census was the first to record African Americans by name. My great and great-great-grandparents' birth years ranged from 1834 to 1867 on the various documents where I located them. This meant half of them were born and lived during slavery, while the other half were born after the American Civil War. My great-grandparents on both sides, fortunately, were born after Emancipation. Their parents were not so lucky and could very well have been born enslaved. Since it was their history that I had decided to start delving into, I was glad they were on board. Digging into their lives would be much harder.

What are Ancestors?

Ancestors are persons from whom one is descended, especially if more remote than a grandparent; a forebear.[6]

I began my search once more on my grandfather's side of the family and returned to his father, Peter Yeldell. I did so for the simple reason that I had such a strong feeling about how he died. This thought was so prevalent in my mind. Lynching predates the formation of the American Republic. It was a practice that was documented during America's early Colonial period. The first lynching I found was a pilgrim by the name of John Billington. The link I found stated the following:

"John Billington, 1630

Arriving with the original band of pilgrims at Plymouth Rock on the Mayflower in 1620, Billington's journey to America had been anything but pleasant. Because Billington was supposedly prone to "blasphemous harangues," ship's captain Miles Standish had the offender's feet and neck tied together as an example of a sin-struck man possessed of a Devil's tongue. Ten years later, Billington became the prime suspect in the murder of John Newcomen -- a neighboring settler done in at close range by a powder-filled blunderbuss. Billington was summarily hanged by an angry mob of pilgrims."[7]

First of all, how do you tie a person's feet and neck together? It seemed that John was a troublemaker that was disliked by all, and his fate was pretty much settled. However, learning this information made me wonder how many lynching's actually happened in the U.S. Although I didn't find the number of lynching's dating back as far as John Billington, I did find the number of lynching's that happened from 1882 to 1968. The Tuskegee Institute (now known as Tuskegee University) did studies on lynchings. It found that from 1882 to 1968 there were 4,745 lynchings of both blacks and whites[8]. Whites were lynched for either helping or supporting blacks or for domestic disputes. This was new to me. I had never heard of white people being lynched. I learned that although all lynchings were not counted, the state with the most lynching's of African Americans was Mississippi, the number of which stands at 539 people. There were ten states whose numbers of lynching victims were over 100 killed. South Carolina was ninth on that list with 156.[9] Another report was done in South Carolina by the Equal Justice Initiative, which found that from 1877 to 1950 a total of 164 lynchings were done in 36 different South Carolina counties.[10] The highest numbers of lynching were in the Edgefield County area. This knowledge lets me know that, while I did not find anything that lead to my great-grandfather Peter being lynched, the possibility of it happening had gone up tremendously. I was just about to hang up my hat on researching lynchings, but there was one more thing that I found that I just couldn't keep to myself. To be honest it should have been taught in history class.

Robert Abbott, a child of former slave captives on St. Simon's Island, Georgia, was founder, editor, and publisher of what became the most successful weekly newspaper in the world called The Chicago Defender. Created in 1905, Robert's newspaper was one of the first to start documenting racial injustices such as rapes, black disenfranchisement, and lynchings. Abbott's reporting became instrumental to the black community. He was a huge supporter of black people leaving the southern states for those in the north. He has been credited for what we know today as the Great Negro Migration. His reporting had helped prompt over 500,000 African Americans to leave the south. He started his paper with 25 cents, which made 300 copies and selling his first edition of the paper from door to door. He pushed his paper across the Mason-Dixon line through the railroad service using Pullman porters and entertainers.[11]

Abbott's newspaper was read in barbershops, family homes, and from church pulpits. The success of the Defender attracted well-known columnists like Walter White and Langston Hughes. The Chicago Defender is still in publication today. This was a fascinating glimpse into African American history, and yet extremely sad. It was fascinating because I know that my mom and grandmother would take the train to Edgefield when they traveled from Washington, DC. My grandmother was probably reading it, which is another way I can feel connected to her. I can read the same newspaper articles she may have very well read herself nearly a century ago. It was sad because here we are in 2017, and this history was sitting right in front of us not being shared or told. This is the type of information that would inspire people, especially those of the same race, to do better; to be better.

There is a quote from Michael Jackson that my daughter has tattooed in Arabic across her shoulder blade, it reads: "study the greats and become greater." It was profound when she told me what it said. It began to make even more sense as I did my research. I started to wonder, was this information kept out of history books on purpose? Someone said, "The best way to hide something from black people is to put it in a book." This was information that I found from reading.

It was very disturbing and I vowed to continue my research and learn more about my people. I stopped the search for Peter Yeldell's death certificate, and his cause of death, and started looking at his mother, Martha. If I thought the information that I found on lynching and Mr. Robert Abbott was a history lesson, Martha's story was going to make my mouth drop to the floor.

The Story of Martha

I wasn't the first person in my family to do research like this. It is said that my mother's second oldest brother John Carlton researched our family as well. Oral history teaches me that per my uncle John, we are descendants of the author Alexandre Dumas and that we come from Haiti. The goal in genealogy is to prove oral history, right or wrong. The woman that I am telling you about now is my 2x great-grandmother Martha Brooks and as I did my research on her I learned she may have been that Haitian connection.

The Caribbean Island was a huge player in the Atlantic Slave trade and traveling there to get slaves was not uncommon. The family that owned Martha was the Brooks family. She seems to have only been owned by them, meaning she wasn't bought from or sold to anyone outside of the family. There is a book called Brooks and Kindred Families which states the first Brooks traveled to the West Indies with his brothers stayed in Virginia for a while and then on to North Carolina. This could have been why my uncle stated, we came from that area because the first Brooks slaves came from the Caribbean Island.

Martha was born in 1834 in South Carolina. I first found her in the 1870 U.S. Federal Census. She had six children: Rebecca (age eighteen) Robert and David (first set of twins, age six), Peter (my great-grandfather, age four), and Thomas and George (second set of twins, age two). The family's surname was listed as Brooks. This threw me for a moment because my great-grandfather Peter's last name was Yeldell in the 1900 and 1910 U.S. Federal Census. Could this be the right family? As far as I knew our name was Yeldell, which was the same name as the family who had enslaved them. Why was their last name Brooks?

I saw them again on the 1880 U.S. Census. This time, Martha's daughter Rebecca had been married and widowed. Her last name now was either Ramey, Ramsey or Rainey. Martha was also cited as being a widow in this census, yet, her last name remained Brooks. Three out of five of her sons were listed as well, Robert, David and my great-granddaddy Peter. There was also a little girl added to the group, and her name was Martha (age six), presumably named for her mother. Strangely enough, she was listed as my 2x great-grandmother's sister.

As I stated above, this census had listed Martha as once having been married, and widowed by 1880. The 1870 census did not allude to any of this. The information given on census records before 1900 were asked, but most did not answer like they did the future census records. So, although the 1880 census stated that she was now a widow, I made the guess that Grandma Martha had been married and widowed after the 1870 census was recorded, as did her daughter Rebecca, and that both of their husbands had died before the 1880 U.S. Census was taken.

Martha was a little confusing. The 1880 census, instead of providing answers, was raising more questions. She had been married and widowed in less than ten years. Two of her sons were not listed and now there is a little girl listed as her sister. However, the straw that broke the camel's back was the fact that David, Robert and Peter's last names were now Yeldell and not Brooks. History teaches us that when slavery ended, newly freed people had the option of keeping the surname of their former owners or taking on a different surname. Why were the boys Yeldells if their mother was a Brooks? Was Martha's maiden name originally Yeldell? Especially since now there has been a possible sister who also had the surname Yeldell? If that was the case, why didn't she change their names sooner?

I went to my mentor and presumed cousin, Candace, with this information. She explained that census takers during that time did not always accurately record information about African Americans. She, along with several other family historians, explained that young Martha was probably my 2nd great-grandmother's daughter, and I agreed. Although the possibility of the young Martha being a daughter, instead of sister, was explained, no one could explain the surname change from Brooks to Yeldell. Martha guided me to questions that may have been impossible to answer.

Questions such as: Where did the Brooks surname come from? Why didn't Martha change their surnames after they were freed? Was it from her marriage or was Martha once enslaved? And the most important question: If she was once enslaved, could she have been the daughter of the slave owner? Those questions bothered me. I knew there was a huge chance that someone in my family was once enslaved, but to find this possibility so soon in my research was, in my opinion, a little fast and somewhat overwhelming.

I kept my focus on Martha and contacted the Tompkins Library in Edgefield to determine if they had any information on a former slave named Martha Brooks. They asked me to provide as much information as I could and, within a few weeks, instead of receiving information from the Tompkins Library, my email was forwarded to the Edgefield County Archives. I received a response from Tricia Price Glenn, the Archivist at the Edgefield archives. The email stated:

> "In 1857, Preston Brooks estate inventory lists Martha, a female slave. She was valued at $1,205, which was very high for that time. If this is your Martha she was obviously considered a prime "breeding" woman. She was sold to Lemuel Brooks that same year. Prior to this time, in 1852 and obviously younger, (before Preston Brooks owned her) she was the property of Whitfield Brooks – Preston's father."

There was confirmation that my 2nd great-grandmother had been enslaved. Who would have thought so early on in my research I would find someone who was held against their will? This was a saddening yet an awesome piece of information. I found the estate records of Whitfield and Preston and learned that when Martha was sold to Lemuel, there were two children sold along with her. This same information was found for me by another genealogist/family historian in a book called Slave Records of Edgefield County by Gloria Lucas[12].

Several thoughts went through my mind after reading that email. However, because I had already prepared myself in case I found such horrors, I was dealing with it. The first thought (sarcastically thinking) was the surname Brooks probably didn't come from her marriage. My second thought stemmed from learning that Martha had not just been enslaved, but was very likely considered a breeder. At the beginning, learning about her being a breeder didn't affect me the way I thought it would have affected other researchers. Instead, I thought, is this the reason why my family is so big? Was it in our genes to be able to have a significant number of children? And have children at such regular intervals? I also realized being a breeder possibly meant that Martha had more children than I had originally counted. As a matter of fact, the two children who were sold with her to Lemuel Brooks could have been her children. I read the email again and this time the phrase a "prime breeding woman" came to light. I wondered why the Edgefield Archivist assumed she was a breeder and a "prime" one at that. I needed to understand this more.

My focus at that point went on what really happened during slavery. One of my fellow family historians said to me that some people didn't believe that slaves were bred. I started my study with a book she directed me to entitle Time on the Cross by Robert Fogel and Stanley Engerman. It is their opinion that:

> "Assertions claiming slave-breeding, sexual exploitation and promiscuity destroyed the black family are myths. The family was the basic unit of social organization under slavery."[13]

These authors argued:

> "It was in the economic interest of planters (slave owners who owned more than 20 slaves) to encourage the stability of slave families and most of them did so." [14]

I then remembered reading the definition of slave breeding in The Making of African American Identity: Vol. I, 1500-1865. It said:

> "Slave breeding – Masters forcibly paired "good breeders" to produce strong children they could sell at a high price. Resistance brought severe punishment, often death." [15]

This was contrary to the opinions of Fogel and Engerman. I went even further and read the WPA Slave Narratives of the 1930s. A former slave by the name of Richard Macks, enslaved in Maryland and interviewed in 1937, said:

> "One time dey sent me on Ol' man Mack Williams' farm here in Jasper County [Georgia]. Dat man would kill you sho. If dat little branch on his plantation could talk it would tell many a tale 'bout folks bein' knocked in de head. I done seen Mack Williams kill folks an' I done seen 'im have folks killed. One day he tol' me dat if my wife had been good lookin', I never would sleep wid her agin 'cause he'd kill me an' take her an' raise chilluns off'n her." [16]

He went on to say:

> "Dey uster [used to] take women away fum dere husbands an' put wid some other man to breed jes' like dey would do cattle. Dey always kept a man penned up an' dey used 'im like a stud hoss." [17]

I did one final search and found a chart explaining the worth of a slave during 1857, the same year Martha was sold to Lemuel Brooks. This chart compared the cost of a slave in 1857 to what a slave would cost if slavery still existed in 1998: [18]

Class	Value in Dollars, 1857	Value in Dollars, 1998
Number 1 men	1250-1450	20,800-24,100
Fair/Ordinary Men	1000-1150	16,700-19,200
Best Boys (Age 15-18)	1100-1200	18,300-20,000
Best Boys (Age 10-14)	500-575	8,300-17,900
Number 1 Women	1050-1225	17,500-20,400
Fair/Ordinary Women	1050-1225	14,200-17,100
Best Girls	500-1000	8,300-16,700
Families	"Sell in their usual proportions"	

According to the chart, Martha was worth the amount of a "Number 1 Woman" and worth more than the amount of a "Fair/Ordinary Man". This is why Tricia called Martha a 'prime breeding' woman. As frightening as that revelation was, my eyes were suddenly opened. I also realized that breeding truly existed. I started to become angry with myself because I wasn't reacting the way I thought I should. I felt I was too nonchalant about this; too accepting. It was a true eye-opener to realize that Martha went through what she went through. I was angry to learn that she had children that I may never find because they were taken and sold, or given away.

Learning that Martha was a breeder brought several things to light. Personally, it provided the realization that I may never learn the name of my 2nd great-grandfather. Not through traditional genealogy practices in terms of following a paper trail. There wouldn't be documentation of this unless the enslaver had written it down somewhere. And what descendant of said enslaver would possibly share such information? I also learned that because she was a breeder she went through many of the atrocities that I read about pertaining to slavery.

- Miscegenation – The interbreeding of individuals considered to be of different racial backgrounds;

- Fancy trade – Female slaves called "fancy maids" were sold at auction into concubinage or prostitution, which was termed the "fancy trade"; and

- Slave breeding – Slave breeding in the United States was a practice of slave ownership that aimed to encourage the reproduction of slaves in order to increase a slaveholder's property and wealth.

Finally, I realized these things didn't just happen to her. There were millions of men and women who went through the same struggles as Martha. It was being brought to my attention that their struggles, not just Martha's struggles, were something I needed to know.

Once again, I was smacked in the face with how much of our history was not being incorporated into schools. Slavery was history that has never been honestly or properly taught. Slavery is mentioned in school only briefly; i.e. it was bad, it happened and now it is over. And the non-teaching of it is getting worse. In Texas, there are schoolbooks that refer to slaves as workers. This reference will lead children to believe that our ancestors were not only paid for the work they did but also came here willingly and not taken from Africa. It is simply a bald-faced lie that will teach children falsehoods about who we are as African Americans, and will further make our children feel that we didn't amount to much before, the only African Americans that are spoken of today such as Martin Luther King, Harriet Tubman, and Frederick Douglas. We were taught that, as a people, we were less than European-descended people. We were taught to believe that, in certain moments in time, we only produced four or five leaders out of the millions of African Americans that were brought here.

It wasn't until the Civil Rights era that schooling about African Americans became more in-depth. Sadly, even then schools taught from the middle of the movement. It was at this moment that I realized my ancestors were introducing me to the hidden history of America, the dark and unspeakable part; the one that all African Americans are told to simply get over. There was something I needed to learn, and eventually, it was going to be taught to me. I was ready to take as much of it in as I could. My research on my family was educating me in a way that school, including higher education, had not. I knew this portion of my lesson from the ancestors was far from over.

    I took some time to regroup and then shared the email from the Edgefield archivist, with my mom. Learning her great-grandmother was enslaved was a horrible discovery, yet to her, it was an expected find. Although I didn't go into the bigger picture, she even understood there were possibly more children out there that we may never know. I told her that because of the information I found about Martha, her surname may not be Yeldell after all. This thought angered my mother. She said to me, in a very indignant tone, *"I AM A YELDELL!"* Most families are very proud of where they came from but being a Yeldell is like being a Rockefeller for either race. To tell her that the possibility that the Yeldell name may not have been her family's original surname challenged who she was at the most basic level. After I explained to my mom what I meant, she wasn't happy. But she understood.

Martha Wasn't Finished

    The information I received was deep and draining. Martha was not just teaching me about her life. She was letting me know what those who were enslaved endured as well. She finally had someone who was listening and she wanted to make sure I got as much as I could. I, in turn, wanted to learn more. Realizing the type of drama that name changing could cause, I started to wonder what others thought about how their family came to have their surnames. I read a blog from another genealogist discussing how his family surname came to be. His question about the surname change mirrored mine.

    I read his blog to get his take on the name change issue. But it was something else that he pointed out that made my heart jump into my throat. Just like me, he found his ancestors with a different name in another document. His research on that second name guided him to the 1850 Slave Schedules of South Carolina. He found his family on the slave schedule, and he pointed out that the enslaved were listed in a unique way. They were listed as a family, with the oldest being first, and then listed down to the youngest.

This was interesting. I knew who Martha's owners were, and had found Martha because of that knowledge in both the 1850 and 1860 slave schedule. However, I never really took notice, or even knew to take notice, of how or in what order they were listed. I went back and viewed the 1850 schedule first. I know you are asking the question: if no name is listed like you said earlier, how do you know you are looking at Martha? It's simple: Martha is the only female slave that matches the age she would have been during that time. My Martha was born about 1834 so in 1850 she would have been about sixteen years old, depending on when her birthday was compared to when the census was taken.

Out of the ninety-three slaves that Whitfield Brooks owned, the one 15-year-old girl listed on the slave schedule was the only one that could have been my 2nd great-grandmother. I checked the 1850 Schedule under Martha's first known slave owner Whitfield Brooks, and the genealogist was right, they were listed in a unique way. They seemed to have been grouped by family. When I viewed the schedule this second time, understanding more in depth what I was looking at, all I could do was grab my mouth. This census image did not just show my 2nd great-grandmother Martha as a teenager anymore. I was now looking at her mother, her father, and her siblings. My heart was racing. I checked the 1860 schedule and it was not like this. Instead, in 1860, they were listed in chronological order. I learned later that the listing depended upon the actual census taker, but looking at what I found in the 1850 schedule was more than exciting and a huge find for me.

I mentioned a book earlier called the Slave Records of Edgefield County. It was purchased for me by my cousin Richard in appreciation of my research. The book is a listing of over fifteen thousand slave names gathered from inventory journals, appraisal journals, wills, estate packages, court records, county deeds, and other miscellaneous records pertaining to slavery. It has the names of all the slaveholders recorded in the Edgefield County area. The book provided, in chart format, the names of the enslaved, a description of the enslaved, the names of the current owners, the names of the new owners, and how much the enslaved were sold for. Martha's first two owners, Whitfield and his son Preston, were both listed in this book, which made Martha appear on two separate pages under two separate owners.

I directed my attention to look at the names of the slaves Whitfield owned in the book and compared them to those on the 1850 slave schedule. Whitfield Brooks died in 1851. Since the information on those he enslaved was gathered from his Will and estate records, the number of slaves recorded on the schedule was not different from the number he owned when he died. Whitfield Brooks owned ninety-three slaves at his death and during the taking of the 1850 Slave Schedule. Now I knew the names of every last one.

According to the book, with the exception of a small group of those enslaved, he did not sell them to anyone outside of the family. In fact, he gave them to his family. The 1850 slave schedule showed Whitfield owned two enslaved families that had three or more children. The book shows the smaller family was given to his son John Hamden Brooks while the larger family (Martha's family) was given to Preston. Martha, however, was for some reason separated from her family and was given to Whitfield's wife Mary, who eventually gave Martha to Preston in what seems to have been an undocumented transaction. My educated guess is that Martha was given to Preston because he was already the owner of her entire family.

However, as you will see later, that may not have been the reason. In short, this extraordinary find gave me the names of my 3rd great-grandparents, and their children: Charles, Crecy, Maria, Becky, Alfred, Sarah, and Edney. These people were the parents and siblings of Martha Brooks. Finding that information was incredible! I did a quick search for Last Will and Testament for both Whitfield and Preston and noticed on Whitfield's three sections were missing. I decided to order the last Will and

Testament for both Whitfield and Preston Brooks, from the Edgefield Archives and stumbled upon something even more pertinent.

Cursive writing during the 1800s was fancier than it was when I was growing up. As a matter of fact, cursive writing isn't even taught in today's teaching. However, because of the way it was written during that time it was very hard to read. During those times, they wrote with the tips of feathers, which were dipped in ink. Dipping in ink allowed for running ink, and smudges, which made reading even more difficult. As hard as it was to read these two Wills, I pushed through and found something very interesting that could probably answer one of the questions I asked early on. The picture above shows a statement that was made by Whitfield Brooks in his Last Will and Testament. Paragraph 12[19] states the following:

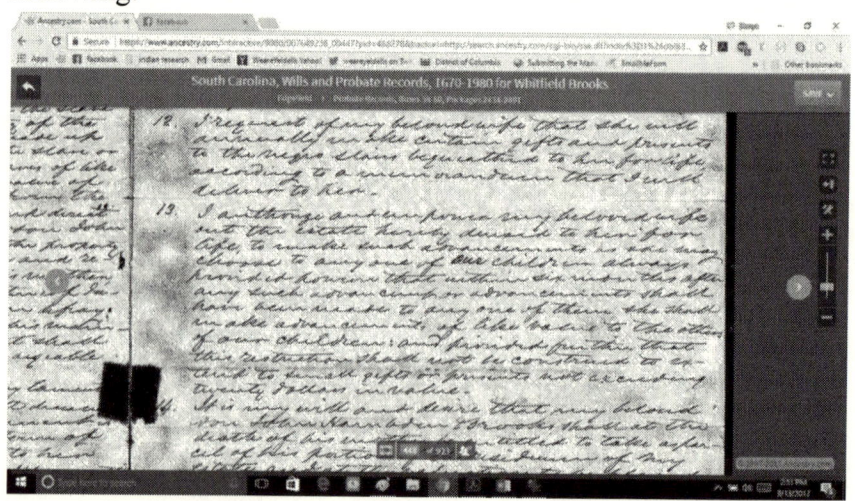

Figure 12 - *Snapshot of Whitfield Brooks Will, Snapshot taken by Donya Williams courtesy of NARA*

"I request of my beloved wife that she will annually make certain gifts and presents to the negro slaves bequeathed to her for life according to a memorandum that I will deliver to her."[20]

I went to the Edgefield Slaves Record book and counted the slaves he gave to his wife. Whitfield gave his wife twenty-nine slaves, eleven of whom were children. Martha was one of those children. It is known that when slaves are mentioned or singled out in the Will, they are special and/or mean something significant to the owner (i.e. lover, child, family member or favored by the owner). Why did he want his wife to give gifts annually to those twenty-nine slaves? Could Martha have actually been his child? The story of Martha was a story I wasn't expecting to find. She had a lot to say and she was nowhere near finished. But in telling me her story, I had to learn the stories of others. I found myself being forced back into American History. There was more research about the form of chattel slavery that was practiced in America that I needed to do.

The House of Bondage

I wasn't really excited to stop my search for family in order to learn more about slavery. This seemed to be important to do, especially where Martha was concerned. She was the ancestor who was guiding me at that moment, and I had to go with her direction. It was March 2013, Women's History Month, and as always, the usual suspects were mentioned for African American Women (Rosa Parks, Harriett Tubman, etc.) Researching had opened my eyes to the realization that we as Americans were not being taught the true history of America. The history as taught in school was heavily edited and in some cases revisionist, history. I decided to use Women's History month to learn about a different Black woman every day. This was my part in enlightening people more accurately about the black experience within the context of American history, so that they could come to their own conclusions. I posted information on my Facebook and Instagram pages about a different woman of a color every day. Most of my information came from a website called Blackpast.org.

Blackpast.org is an online reference center makes available a wealth of materials on African American history in one central location on the Internet. These materials include an online encyclopedia of over 4,000 entries, the complete transcript of more than 300 speeches by African Americans, other people of African ancestry, and those concerned about race, given between 1789 and 2016, over 140 full text primary documents, bibliographies, timelines and six gateway pages with links to digital archive collections, African and African American museums and research centers, genealogical research websites, and more than 200 other website resources on African American and global African history.[21] The information from this site was incredible. I retrieved a name every day with something interesting that I had never learned before. One day I chose a woman by the name of Octavia V. Rogers Albert.

Octavia was a 19th-century author and religious leader, who was born 1853 in Oglethorpe, Georgia into slavery. Although she was a former slave, she published a book called The House of Bondage, or, Charlotte Brooks and Other Slaves, Original and Life Like, As They Appeared in Their Old Plantation and City Slave Life; Together with Pen-Pictures of the Peculiar Institution, with Sights and Insights into Their New Relations as Freedmen, Freemen, and Citizens – or House of Bondage for short. There was a moment in time after the civil war where blacks and whites lived in a type of Utopia. We went to school, we held high offices, we were as close to equal as we were ever going to be. This was the world of the Reconstruction Era.

The Reconstruction era is dated 1865 – 1877. It was during this time that the 13th, 14th, and 15th Amendments were added to the Constitution, which moved part of the fight between the North and South from the battlefield to the political arena. The 13th Amendment abolished slavery, the 14th Amendment grants birth rights (meaning if you are born here than you are considered an American) and the 15th Amendment grants voting rights. Each one was specifically crafted for those who were once enslaved to be treated as equals. With this equality, African Americans caught up with their once enslavers at an extremely fast pace. It was during this time that African Americans became elected officials, were educated not just by reading and writing but in higher learning as well. We were the founders of schools and were able to patent inventions for the betterment of America. In that short period of time, we became doctors, held high positions in the military and more. This became too much for the once enslavers and when the last northern army left the south the degradation of African Americans began again.

Octavia lived in that Utopic world. She enrolled at Atlanta University and, three years later, she began teaching in Montezuma, Georgia. While there she met her soon-to-be husband A.E.P Albert. Octavia's husband became an ordained minister in the Methodist Episcopal Church. In 1888, they moved to Louisiana. Octavia's husband was a minister in the town of Houma, Louisiana. Due to his status as a minister, which was part of the newly burgeoning black middle class of former freedmen and women, it was not common for women to have professional positions of their own. This made Octavia a stay at home mom and a known community and religious leader.

It was not uncommon for the people of the community to stop by and share stories of their time during slavery with her. The stories that were shared made up her book the House of Bondage. It was during those moments of sharing that Octavia met a woman named Charlotte Brooks. Charlotte seemed to have been the main character in the book. Although the stories came from different formerly enslaved people, the bulk of the stories came from Charlotte. She told Octavia stories not just of herself, but of those that lived with and around her. Originally the stories were first published after the death of Octavia, in the Louisiana newspaper the South Western Christian Advocate. Her chapters were published in serial format, in a manner similar to how other contemporary authors such as Charles Dickens were publishing their stories. As soon as the series ended, her husband was bombarded with request to turn the stories into a book. To honor his wife, and mother of his only daughter, the book was then published in 1890.

Here is my hope, as you have been reading this, your thought process is changing and you are learning nothing is coincidental. If this is the case, then the name Charlotte Brooks struck a chord with you just as it did me. After reading about Octavia and her book, I had to have it. I needed to find out if Charlotte was related to my Martha. I immediately went to Amazon.com and ordered it. Let me just say if there was ever a book that should be read by every person in the world, this was it. From the first sentence in the introduction that read, "THE story of slavery never has been and never will be fully told" to the heartwarming reunion between

Charlotte's friend Aunt Jane and her son, this book was amazing from beginning to end.

Reading this book, I was able to see a correlation between the late 1800s, through the several different stories as recounted in Olivia's book, and the story of Martha Brooks. There were statements that we have heard in the 21st Century that I never knew came from as far back as the 19th Century. If I could, I would rewrite that book within this book, but then it would no longer be about the research of my family. Instead, I will share one story that Charlotte told that could have been something that Martha herself possibly experienced.

The Story of Ella

Charlotte would seem to have visited Octavia almost every day. She told her stories about how she was separated from her family in Virginia, and how she lost her children. Charlotte didn't mention the names of her slave owners or their plantations, but I think they were purposely omitted by Octavia. When Charlotte shared her stories, the book would refer to the ex-slave owners as marsters/mistress, or to the plantations as the state she was currently living in. The story I am about to share starts with Octavia asking if there was ever anything good to say about Charlotte's former master.

> **Octavia**: "But Aunt Charlotte, have you nothing good to tell? Did your master never show any sympathy for his slaves?"
>
> **Charlotte**: "My dear child, if you believe me, I never got one dollar from my marster in my life. After rolling was over he would get big jugs of whisky and make us all drink at his house door, but after that nothing more but hard work and rough treatment from one year's end to the other.
>
> I want to tell you about poor Ella, old mistress's house-servant. She was only twelve years old. Ella's mother did not live with her. Mistress had no more feeling for her than she had for a cat. She used to beat her and pull her ears till they were sore. She

would crack her on the head with a key or any thing she could get her hands on till blood would ooze out of the poor child's head. Mistress's mother give Ella to her, and when Ella got to be about eighteen mistress got jealous of her and old marster. She used to punish Ella all sorts of ways. Sometimes she tied her up by her thumbs. She could do nothing to please mistress. She had been in the habit of tying Ella up, but one day she tied her up and left her, and when she went back she found Ella dead. She told old marster she did not intend to kill her, that she only wanted to punish her. Mistress and marster did not live good after she killed Ella, for a long time. Poor Ella! I don't know where she is to-day. She was a Catholic. You could always see her with her beads and cross in her pocket. She is in purgatory, I reckon; for the Catholics say the priest can hold mass and get any body out for so much money. But nobody held mass for Ella, and so she will have to stay in purgatory.

But, I tell you, I believe there is only two places for us--heaven and torment. If we miss heaven we must be forever lost."

Octavia: "Yes, Aunt Charlotte, that's the teaching of the Bible."

Charlotte: "Aunt Jane used to tell us, too, that the children of Israel was in Egypt in bondage, and that God delivered them out of Egypt; and she said he would deliver us."[22]

Who was Ella to the mistress or the master? Reading this story, several scenarios came to mind. Ella could have been a child of the mistress's father. This could be why the mistress's mother gave the child to her and why Ella had no feeling for her at all. In other words, Ella could have been her mistress's half-sister. What I think to be obvious was when Ella turned eighteen, her relationship with the master was close enough to make his wife jealous. What could have done that, but to have meant that Ella was probably the master's sexual partner? It would explain why he and his wife never lived in the same way after Ella was killed. As I read the entire book, I never confirmed if Charlotte was related to Martha. But who knows? What I did know was that scenario with Ella could have easily been my 2x great-grandmother Martha.

I did more research on white women and how they were with the enslaved children held within their family and received some information I was not expecting. A friend of mine shared a video she found of a woman named Dr. Joy DeGruy Leary. I was going to save Dr. Leary for another portion of this book, but with all research, you always find more things than what you are really looking for. Dr. Leary posted a video of herself in London in 2008 about a subject she studied for years called PTSD/PTSS a.k.a Post Traumatic Slave Disorder/Post Traumatic Slave Syndrome. According to Dr. Leary PTSD/PTSS is the effect that occurred after slavery to both black and white people. Dr. Leary's research discusses how generations of slavery, for the enslaved and their enslavers, still carries an effect on people today. The video is called Post Traumatic Syndrome by Dr. Joy DeGruy Leary. In section 50:23 on the video, Dr. Leary discusses a law that was written in 1669 called the Casual Killing Act. To understand why the law was written you should know what the law says:

Casual Killing Act

"Whereas the only law in force for the punishment of refractory servants resisting their master, mistress or overseer cannot be inflicted upon negroes, nor the obstinacy of many of them by other than violent means suppressed, Be it enacted and declared by this grand assembly, if any slave resist his master (or others by his masters order correcting him) and by the extremity of the correction should chance to die, that his death shall not be considered a felony, but the master (or that other person appointed by the master to punish him) be acquit from molestation, since it cannot be presumed that malice existed (which alone makes murder a felony) [or that

Comes to The Light

anything] should induce any man to destroy his own estate."[23]

In short, this law gave slave masters, or those that received an order from an enslaver were given the right to beat a slave to death and not be charged with a crime. As horrifying as this act was, Dr. Leary went one step further to find out what slaves were being beaten to death and by whom. Her discovery was mind-blowing. Dr. Leary discovered that white women were beating black children to death. So, when the mistress had been terrorizing poor Ella when the enslaved girl reached the age of twelve, she was never held responsible for her actions. She was never held responsible for the murder of Ella. Martha had done it! She had introduced me to the world of slavery. The constant pain, anguish, despair, and heartbreak enslaved people had to go through. What was most sad about what I had found is that this wasn't even the half of it. Octavia said it best when she said,

> "NONE but those who resided in the South during the time of slavery can realize the terrible punishments that were visited upon the slaves. Virtue and self-respect were denied them."[24]

I took so much more than just the stories from the book when it came to the American institution of chattel slavery. I learned that what we saw in movies of who we were as a people, and how we spoke, was not true. The old Negro dialect had us speaking in broken sentences and mispronounced words. When, in fact, those who were enslaved spoke more or less in the manner that we do now. After reading the House of Bondage, I realized it wasn't just the horrific stories that Martha wanted me to know. She wanted me to learn my power, and that we didn't just become smart after the Civil Rights movement.

We were enslaved, malnourished, made to feel inferior and kept illiterate for hundreds of years. How scary was it to the once dominant race to watch the same people who had been treated as property become free? How was it for them to see the formerly enslaved become educators, hold high political office, become respected and prominent civic leaders, successful and wealthy business people, property owners, or high ranking military officers within a decade? Our intelligence scared the crap out of them.

Now that I got what she wanted me to know, I eventually found more of Martha's descendants who turned out to be the children of my great-grandfather Peter's brother David. In fact, I found several of David's descendants who connected us to the **Roundtrees, Ruckers** and **Speaks** families. After confirming our relationship through DNA, I shared with them our connection and the fascinating story of our shared ancestor. I knew that Martha was happy that her children were being brought back together after all these years. But there is one more person, she wanted to tell me about. Since I knew who her owners were, she wanted me to look at them. But instead of me focusing on the first or last person that owned her, I was being pushed towards Whitfield's son, Preston Brooks.

Slave Owner Preston S. Brooks

My grandmothers were becoming my favorite people in the world. Even though I had never met them, I felt like I knew them. The more I researched, the more confident I became. With Martha, I was learning her life and the things she may have gone through while being a slave. She had pointed me towards her second owner, Preston Brooks instead of his father, or her last enslaver, Lemuel Brooks. Lemuel was a cousin of Preston Brooks. Lemuel would enslave Martha from 1857 to 1863 until the time of the Emancipation Proclamation was signed.

Some of those who were enslaved didn't know they were freed once the Emancipation Proclamation was signed. I believe Martha did know. Martha signed up to be counted in the first census that African Americans were counted and listed by name like every other American citizen in 1870. Even though the 1870 and 1880 census listed Martha as unable to read or write, it was a gut feeling that made me feel otherwise. Not all African Americans were counted in 1870 how did she know the importance of being counted?

Martha was reared around intelligent people and just because a person is not physically taught how to read and write doesn't mean they can't learn it on their own. We were not deaf and dumb, we were survivors. If she was the child of someone in the Brooks family, she may have been privy to conversations that other enslaved people were not which taught her more than one may have thought. I know that this was a gut feeling that I had and that it could not be proven with paper, but it was all that I had and given what she had gone through and survived it was enough for me. It was time to learn what she wanted me to know about Preston.

Preston Brooks was born on the Roseland plantation 5 August 1819 to Whitfield Brooks and Mary Parsons **Carroll Brooks**. This is the same plantation I believe Martha worked on. Preston came from a long line of soldiers and patriots. He fought, and was a Captain, in the Mexican War, while both his father Whitfield and his grandfather Zachariah fought in battles that were part of the American Revolution. There is not much information on Preston as a child. As a matter of fact, the first account of Preston came from a time when he attended college. It is very brief but it tells you the type of person he was.

Just days before his graduation from South Carolina College (now known as University of South Carolina) in 1838, a story was passed around that one of his brothers was arrested and being abused by the police. This angered Preston so much that he grabbed some pistols, went to the jailhouse, and threatened the officers. Although they were able to disarm him, the fact that he did something like this was amazing. There were other incidents during his time in college, but the trustees of the school had had enough. This incident stopped him from receiving his degree. Nevertheless, he went on to practice law. He was admitted to the South Carolina Bar in 1845 and practiced law in Edgefield, South Carolina while being a member of the State House of Representatives.

It was during this time that he participated in a duel that went down as one of the top 100 duels in the world. We all know the statement "the apple doesn't fall far from the tree"; well it fits in this situation. The reason for the duel was quite simple. Anonymously written letters were sent to an Edgefield newspaper.

The contents of these letters offended a man named Louis Trezevant Wigfall. In return, Wigfall demanded to know who the author of said letters was. He learned that the author was Preston's father, Whitfield. Defending the slights against his character, which he perceived arose from the publication of these letters, Wigfall challenged the 65-year-old Whitfield Brooks to a duel.

Whitfield of course declined, which made him even more enraged. Wigfall decided to go even further in what appeared to be an attempt to anger Whitfield enough to accept his challenge. Wigfall printed a pamphlet and posted it on the doors of the Edgefield County Court House, one of the busiest and most public areas on the Edgefield square. The pamphlet declared Whitfield Brooks to be a coward. Wigfall then stated that if anyone tried to take the note down, he would kill them on the spot.

Wigfall was good friends with Whitfield's brother-in-law, Chancellor Carroll. Carroll knew that his brother-in-law was not a coward, but just too old to participate in such activities. One day while Wigfall was in the Edgefield square Carroll decides to pull Wigfall to the side to try and talk Wigfall into taking the note down. Wigfall refused. Like the gentlemen, they were, and in honor of his brother-in-law, Chancellor Carroll invited Wigfall to duel. While that conversation was taking place, Thomas Byrd, a grandson of Whitfield, walked towards the courthouse up the steps and with every intention proceeded to tear the pamphlet down. He had his hand on the corner of the note when Wigfall, brandishing two pistols, said to Byrd:

"Byrd if you touch that I shall kill you."[25]

Byrd's response:

"I reckon two can play at killing."[26]

And while making the comment, Byrd proceeded to take the note down. However, he only managed to remove a small corner of the note, because Wigfall had shot him directly in the heart. Byrd fell dead, and Wigfall continued his conversation with Chancellor Carroll.

There was no action taken towards Wigfall. I guess it was to his right to react as he did. This speaks to the culture of Edgefield at that time. What had begun as a quarrel between two men, Louis Wigfall and Whitfield Brooks, had now increased to four, with the inclusion of Byrd, who was now dead, and Carroll. When Wigfall and Carroll met up on Walton's Island, they were standing the required ten paces apart from one another, waiting for the word to fire. When the word was finally given, and they fired on each other, they both missed and the duel was called a draw. They shook hands and left the scene.

When they had traveled two miles down the road they were met by Whitfield's, son Preston. Preston had come home from the Mexican War and was infuriated with the recent events that had involved his father. Wigfall had attacked not only his father but killed his nephew, Thomas Byrd. Preston wasted no time in challenging Wigfall to a duel right on the spot. The rest of the story is best told by the reporter at the *Evening Star* in Washington, DC.

Excerpt from "SOUTH CAROLINA DUELS

Reminisences of the Code Told in the Capitol

They had just ridden 2 miles from and were entering the little town of Hamburg, across the river from Augusta, when they were met by Preston Brooks. He had been absent from home during the previous difficulties and had just heard of them. But the fiery Brooks lost no time in challenging Wigfall to another duel, and it was arranged then and there that they immediately return to Walton's Island and fight to the death. Both were brave and reckless young fellows and each wanted the blood of his opponent. They returned. Ten paces were stepped off and the combatants took their places. Not a muscle in either quivered as they stood awaiting the signal to fire. It was given. Two triggers were pressed at the same instant. Only one report was heard, but both men fell. The two shots were simultaneous and each man had a bullet hole through his thigh. Neither could stand to shoot again."[27]

This, of course, was just one variation of the story, but this version of the story was told with so much imagination, I had to share it. For the most part, however, it was accurate, with the exception of the number of shots that had been fired, and when this second duel had taken place. They had fired more than once, and Wigfall had actually been shot through both of his thighs. Preston had been shot in the hip. Both were severely injured, but they both recovered. Wigfall eventually moved to Texas while Preston continued to make his home in Edgefield. By 1853, Preston was elected as a Democrat to the 33rd and 34th Congresses. His actions while in Congress would make his name, although infamous, go down in history.

During the 1800s the Republican and the Democratic parties were not as we recognize them to be today. Most African Americans feel that today's Republican Party is not supportive of African American equality, while the Democratic Party shows periods of active support. During the Antebellum and Reconstruction Eras, the defining characteristics of both parties, as we see them today, were reversed. The Republican Party supported the belief that slavery was wrong and fought for it to be abolished.

The Democratic Party fought to maintain the institution of chattel slavery. Preston was unapologetically a Democrat. Some American history books teach the story of how the abolitionist Charles Sumner was physically assaulted on the floor of the U.S. Senate. The political caricature that you see, drawn by J.L. Magee in 1856, depicts a northern congressman being beaten by a southern congressman. It was a reenactment of the events that occurred after Charles

Figure 13 - Southern Chivalry Argument versus Club's Photo credit New York Public Library Creator John L. Magee

Sumner gave his thoughts on an occurrence in Kansas. History buffs, or those who paid attention in school, may remember learning about a bill called the Kansas-Nebraska Act. This bill was beneficial to the continuation of slavery in areas that slavery had been banned. According to the book

"To Free a Family: The Journey of Mary Walker"

"In January 1854, Congress passed and the president signed the Kansas-Nebraska Bill, which voided the Missouri Compromise of 1820 and the Compromise of 1850, and allowed slavery to enter the territory from which it had been barred since 1787."[28]

Charles Sumner (R - Massachusetts), an abolitionist who fought against slavery along with Lincoln, was beaten because of a two-day speech he gave on the Senate floor concerning this bill. **"The Crime Against Kansas**: *The Apologies for the Crime; The True Remedy"*[29] was written and recited by Senator Sumner because of several events that occurred during a time when the North and South were fighting over the question of where slavery would be permitted within the Union. The Kansas-Nebraska Act made it possible for the Kansas and Nebraska territories to be open to slavery. People from the North were certain that slavery could return to an area where it had been banned for over 30 years.[30]

Violence broke out in the Kansas Territory and the issue was placed front and center in Congress. Sumner's speech, which was given on 19-20 May 1856, verbally attacked two of Senator Preston Brooks' fellow colleagues, Senator Andrew Butler (D – South Carolina), later said to be Preston's uncle, and Senator Stephen A. Douglas (D – Illinois.). Senator Brooks (D – South Carolina) was present for the reading of that speech. The speech was stirring, to say the least, and very degrading to the two above mentioned senators, and to the state of South Carolina. Preston was not fond of this speech, and for two days he thought about the best way to approach Senator Sumner. In different versions, I have read regarding this account, one stated that Brooks spoke with Rep. Laurence Keitt (South Carolina) and wondered if he should challenge Sumner to a duel, like a gentleman, or do something more drastic and dramatic. Keitt said:

> "Dueling was for gentlemen of equal social standing. In his view, Sumner was no gentleman; no better than a drunkard, due to his supposedly coarse and insulting language toward Butler."[31]

On 22 May 1856, Senator Brooks made his decision on how to approach Senator Sumner. While Senator Sumner sat at his desk, Senator Brooks walked up to him and said:

> "You've libeled my state and slandered my white-haired old relative, Senator Butler, and I've come to punish you for it"[32.]

Senator Brooks, who was already known for having a violent temperament, proceeded to strike Sumner several times over the head with a metal-tipped gutta-percha cane. His colleagues, Laurence Keitt and Virginia Rep. Henry A. Edmundson, held back the other senators who were present. Keitt held them back at gunpoint. Wielding his cane, and shouting

> "Let them alone, God damn you".[33]

Preston Brooks hit Mr. Sumner so often, and so violently, that the cane eventually broke. He wrote a letter back to his home sharing with his brother what he did just in case there was some backlash. Congress needed two-thirds of the votes to remove Preston from public office. They did not get the votes they needed. However, he voluntarily resigned from office and, in lieu of his actions, received a $300 dollar fine. Laurence Keitt was censured for his participation.

The North's reaction to Brooks' outburst generated a much-needed spark in the Republican Party. Alexander McClure, a journalist and an active member of the Pennsylvania Republican party, said:

> "By great odds the most effective deliverance made by any man to advance the Republican Party was made by the bludgeon of Preston S. Brooks."[34]

In a letter addressed to Abraham Lincoln, Senator Lyman Trumball stated:

"The feeling here is much better than some months ago. The outrage upon Sumner & the occurrences in Kansas, have helped us vastly."[35]

However, Preston Brooks' actions were viewed in an entirely different way in the south. Mr. Brooks, my ancestors' owner, had the full support of the southern states. To show their support, several events were held in his honor. The Meeting of the Secessionists of South Carolina at Ninety-Six, an event held to honor Mr. Brooks, was held 1 November 1856. During this meeting, the Honorable Preston S. Brooks was presented with goblets of silver and gold and canes that replicated the same cane he used to beat Mr. Charles Sumner. During this event, he gave a speech expressing his full support of seceding from the Union and doing whatever necessary to keep slavery going. He wrote:

"I tell you, fellow citizens, from the bottom of my heart, that the only mode, which I think available for meeting it is just to tear the Constitution of the United States, trample it under foot, and form a southern confederacy, every state of which will be a slaveholding State. I believe it, as I stand in the face of my maker—I believe it on my responsibility you as your honored representative that the only available means of making that hope effective is to cut asunder the bonds that tie us together, and take our separate positions in the family of nations. These are my opinions. They have always been my opinions. I have been a disunionist from the time I could think".[36]

Preston was not a supporter of the Constitution and he never held his tongue when it came to his feelings about the existence of slavery and seceding from the Union. Although Preston resigned from his Senate seat for what he did to Charles Sumner, South Carolina re-elected him. Preston died in Washington, DC from croup — any infection of the larynx or trachea, accompanied by a hoarse, ringing cough; difficulty breathing.[37] His death was advertised in all of the papers varying different opinions from north to south. ***The Yorkville Enquirer*** of York, South Carolina wrote:

> "Upon the reception in Columbia, of the melancholy intelligence, by telegraph, of the death of the late Preston S. Brooks, the Mayor of the city immediately ordered the great bell to be tolled, in respect to his memory. The exercises of the South Carolina College were suspended, and the chapel bell gave forth the mournful tone which signified the departure of one whose memory the whole state will reverence while memory lasts. The students of the College held a meeting, at which was adopted a series of resolutions setting forth the sorrow of the meeting for the of the Hon. P.S. Brooks, as that of a patriot and a true friend to the South Carolina College."[38]

While papers further north, like ***The Daily Dispatcher*** from Richmond, VA. Wrote:

> "The Sudden death of Preston S. Brooks, by one of the most virulent and painful diseases that afflict humanity, can scarcely fail to impress the public as a signal instance of Divine retribution for atrocious and peculiar crime a bold and arrogant man while yet boasting of his dastardly outrage – while yet swaggering with the barbaric honors showered upon him by a brutalized constituency – his lips still quivering with threats against the friends and associates of his victim – is seized by the throat by an invisible and irresistible grasp, and strangled to death. He dies, says a dispatch from Washington, a horrid death, suffering intensely, and endeavoring to tear his own throat open to get breath."[39]

In 1860, with the election of Abraham Lincoln, South Carolina seceded from the Union on the 20th of December in that same year. Preston's unapologetic actions towards Sumner and his outspoken eagerness to secede from the Union is said by some historians and journalist were the catalyst that started the Civil War.

What a story Martha had guided me too! I can only imagine what she heard while being a part of such a family. She had a first-hand knowledge of his ways, his protective nature of his family and more. One of Preston's 4x great-grandchildren shares DNA with my mom. This means my mother and I are blood relations to the Preston and Whitfield Brooks family line. This name increased my list of surnames to research on my maternal grandfather's side by two: Brooks, and possibly Carroll (Carroll is on Preston's mother's side of the family)

I've often been asked how I feel about Preston being my relative. To be honest, I don't know for certain if Preston is my 2nd great-grandfather, Martha's half-brother, or her father. What I do know is that he was a controversial figure who reminded me of the attitudes that some of the men and women in my family have. His connection to me strangely was not a surprise. Instead, I started to understand more, not just about me, but more about my family.

Figure 14 - One-hundred and thirty-nine-year-old Bible, Photo taken by Donya Williams

Chapter 6 – Ezra Adams And Liberty Springs Baptist Church

Martha's story was amazing. But it was time to take a step back from her. She wasn't the only one with a story that needed to be told. When I look back on what I have found so far, I had gone from one surname (Yeldell) and added 16 more names. I decided to stick with my grandfather's side of the family and began my search with Jefferson's maternal grandparents, Ezra **Adams** and J. **Holloway**-Adams. They were the parents of Jefferson's mother Katie Adams Yeldell. Ezra and his wife were first seen in the 1870 census with their first three children: Rhody, Elvira, and Caty (Katie), my grandfather's mother.

Katie was three years old, while her two sisters were ten and five. By 1880, Ezra and J. Holloway had two more children, this time boys: Ellerape and Gairy, who were also ten and five when this census was taken. Just like Jefferson Yeldell and Annie Mae Senior, Ezra and his wife had a pattern of having children every 18 months to 2 years. This could have been where my family's pattern of having children like clockwork came from.

If you notice, I am calling my 2nd great-grandmother J. I am calling her J because she seemed to be the victim of the worst case of misspelled name and incorrect information I have ever come across in my family. This could cause a huge problem in researching whereas I might not be able to find her due to the constant misspelling of her name. The 1870 census record taker wrote what looked to be "Jayary", a name that no one was able to pronounce or understand. By 1880, the name spelling had changed again to "Jain S".

As I stated previously, I research with other people who also happen to be my family. Since none of us could figure out her name, we decided to call her by the letter "J" when referring to her. However, it wasn't until the 1900 census that her name was spelled in an entirely different way. So different that it was another name altogether, which made us believe she had died and Ezra had married another woman. Her name was Aimie. This made me, and the others think that "J" had definitely died and this was indeed a different woman, a second wife.

I looked at the 1910 Census and saw Ezra with the same woman from the 1900 census, but her name was now spelled, Amy. What confirmed my thoughts that she was a second wife was the 1910 census listing the number two by Ezra's marital status. When a number is listed next to the marital status, it means the person has been married more than once. Ezra had the number two next to his marital status, indicating a second marriage. As far as I was concerned, Aimie/Amy was definitely my step 2x great-grandmother. She and Ezra had been married for 20 years. Wait, 20 years? This was impossible. He had been married to Aimie for 36 years in the 1900 census. If he was married to "J" from 1870 to at least 1880, and he married Amy in 1890 - by 1910 it would make 20 years. Yet, this count was rolling backward. Was I to assume that two different census takers were just plain wrong?

This was the biggest, the most confusing mess I had ever come across. I started to wonder if "J" Holloway-Adams was also Amy Adams. I checked the death certificates of the children and had no help from this. Out of their eight children, I found five death certificates. Three death certificates listed a Joycie/Joysia/Joycie Ann. One death certificate listed an Amy Jones, and the last one had no mother listed at all. With none of the records proving anything, either way, I was unsure of what to believe. I had also found the death certificate of Amy Adams. It was there that I learned that Amy's mother was Isabella Settles and that Isabella had been the wife of Wade Holloway.

Although this didn't confirm if these two women were one in the same person, I did find my possible 3x great-grandparents. I just didn't know if they were my biological great-grandparents or my step great-grandparents. Joyce/Amy was confusing, and I didn't know if all eight children were Joyce's, or if at least one of them was Amy's. The only other way I could prove anything definitively was to have descendants of the children to test for DNA. Since I didn't have access to living descendants at the moment, and I knew that Joyce was definitely a Holloway, I took the decision to make Joyce and Amy the same woman. The rest of my family agreed. At that point, I directed my focus more on Ezra. Focusing on him didn't help me in narrowing down the information I needed for J./Amy Holloway. It did, however, help me find something even greater.

I was given information about a church called Liberty Springs. Tonya Browder Ray, who is the head of the African American genealogist research library in Edgefield, wrote a book on the African American Churches of Edgefield. The book said:

> "The Liberty Springs Baptist Church was founded in 1873 with Brothers Jack Holloway and Ezra Adams as our church leaders. Reverend W.M. Peterson (Son of Springfield Church) served as the pastor of Liberty Spring from its infancy to his death in 1934."[40]

I was so excited to find something like this. I also read, the church received its first Bible on October 5, 1878, which we still have today.[41] This was exciting because Bibles can carry genuinely invaluable information, such as family births, deaths, and marriages. I called, spoke with a Gwen Harrison, and asked her if there was any writing in the Bible. She did not know.

She also didn't know how Ezra and Jack could be brothers, but I knew and explained how I had reached the conclusion that they were relations through marriage: Ezra had married Jack's sister. There was so much potential with a Bible this old. I realized I had reached a point where I needed to travel to Edgefield. Questions started to form in my head: what would I find, what would I see, but most importantly, how would I react to being there? One thing I did know was that this trip would be life-changing.

My Journey to Edgefield, S.C.

Have you ever seen the movie National Treasure starring Nicholas Cage? The character that Nicolas Cage played was a man who was told as a young boy a story about a huge treasure. When he is old enough, he spends his adult life looking - or better yet trying to prove - the oral stories that were told to him about this treasure. What made the hunt worth his while was the memory of his paternal grandfather reciting to him that his ancestor was the key to finding this lost treasure. He told him:

"The secret lies with Charlotte."[42]

Well when he finally found Charlotte, which was a boat, that boat led him to another clue, which led him to another clue, and so on. He went through several clues until he finally found the treasure.

In the over twenty years that I have been researching my family, I have been told all manner of wonderful stories about my ancestors. Those stories were clues to finding my treasure. Researching my family is just like the movie National Treasure. When I went to see that 136-year-old bible, words cannot express the excitement that was coursing through me. I was excited and nervous at the same time because this bible could very well hold the answers to several important questions, like what was grandma J's real name, or when was grandma J born, and when did she die? Since she was married to one founder and the sister of another, there was bound to be some information in this book.

When I arrived in Edgefield, Sheila and two of her cousins, Nafeez and Daisy Boo (that was my nickname for Daisy), took me to Liberty Springs to meet with Ulysses and his cousin. They were going to show me the bible. I was anxious to see that bible and, when we got there, it was on the podium. When I walked up to it, the bible looked brand new and nowhere near 136-years-old. The reason for that turned out to be a simple one: it had been rebound. Nevertheless, you could smell the history of it because of the original old pages. I opened the book and didn't see anything apart from the printed text on the pages. There were no marriage dates, no death dates; nothing. Although the book didn't provide me with any information just knowing I had my hands on something that my 2x great-grandfather once touched was good enough for me. I didn't leave empty-handed. Ulysses' cousin was going to get me in touch with the family of the secretary of the church, which I knew would lead me to another clue. This wasn't the end it was just the beginning. Edgefield was just getting started.

Going to see the bible was not my first visit to Edgefield. I had gone there once before as a presenter for the Southern Studies Showcase, a genealogical conference thrown by the Old Edgefield District Genealogical Society and the Edgefield Civic League. The Southern Studies Showcase was a two-day event that brought genealogical and historical societies from all over South Carolina and parts of Georgia to the town of Edgefield[43]. Why do they come to Edgefield? They come to Edgefield because it's the best-kept secret in American History.

Unlike most southern cities during or after the Civil War or War Between the States as those in the south call it, Edgefield for some reason had been one of the few places that were spared from being burned down and destroyed. Since this did not happen, they were able to keep ALL of their records. Having all of its records made Edgefield the prime spot for research, particularly for African Americans whose families were sold, bought or simply born in the area. This town had everything from deeds, to wills, to land records and personal estate records; and they were all available for research. In so many words, Edgefield is the equivalent of a gold mine for people who were researching this town.

For African American researchers, the information they have is a huge help in finding their families. As you learn about Edgefield, you begin to learn about the colonies. South Carolina was the 10th colony formed, and one out of the four largest slaveholding states. Anywhere from 40 to 60 percent of the

Africans who were brought to America during the slave trade entered through ports in the Lowcountry[44]. As I did my research, I was learning that a large portion of the enslaved was sold on the same courthouse steps that Wigfall had shot and killed Thomas Byrd. If they weren't sold on the courthouse steps, the enslaved had certainly traveled through Edgefield. Since I was there during the Southern Showcase, I tried to gather as many records together as I could. All the research I had done so far had been done via the National Archives, ordering from the Tomkins library, and using other online resources. I wanted to take full advantage of the weekend and get in as much research as possible.

Traveling to Edgefield was a big deal for me. As far as I knew, no one in my family had been there since my grandfather was laid to rest there in 1964. I got in touch with my cousin Ulysses Freeman, who I found the year before, and told him that I was finally visiting. He insisted that I stay with him. There isn't an airport in Edgefield, so my plan was to fly to Greenville, South Carolina, rent a car from there, and drive the rest of the way. When I picked up my rental, I knew this would be a trip I would never forget because written on the rental agreement holder were the words, "your journey begins here". It was right, and I was ready. It was a chance for me to see where my ancestors had lived; attend the church my family attended, and meet the people that may have known or knew some of my people.

I shared my research experience with my friends and family on Facebook all the time, and also through my blog, so they all knew how excited I was to finally go to Edgefield. I posted a message that I had landed in Greenville, South Carolina and was picking up the rental car. Several people commented. There was one comment, however, that stood out from the rest. My newly found cousin, Ken Yeldell, who is the great-grandson of my grandfather's brother Gary, made me cry by saying "welcome home cuz". He was right. This was a homecoming for me. That was the first tear of many that I would shed while on this pilgrimage. The ride to Edgefield was about an hour and a half long. I knew I was almost there when I got to highway 25.

Highway 25

Highway 25 is the road to Edgefield and riding down that road was an experience in itself. It is lined with trees as tall as the Washington Monument on each side. As you ride down Highway 25 and take in the scenery, something within the trees started to grab my attention. I started to see a bright light within the trees, almost like a reflection. As I kept driving I realized it was a reflection that was coming from the sun shining on several different tin like objects. I realized that the tin like objects were the roofs of old homes that had been taken over by the trees. They weren't just any old homes, but shacks with metal rooftops, possibly old slave quarters or places where my ancestors may have once lived.

As I rode down Highway 25 and saw those houses, I don't know if it was my imagination, but here is where things became creepy and you may start questioning my sanity. I started to see people running, hiding; or mothers calling their children in for the night. Yeah, I know you are like "really Donya" but I know what I saw, and seeing that reminded me of another oral story that was told to me by my mother. She said she didn't travel to Edgefield to bury her dad, but her sister told her that as they were leaving Edgefield, right at the line of Edgefield and Greenwood, she looked back and saw her father waving goodbye. Now maybe I was having my own experience, and I started to wonder about those homes: who lived in them; and how many of them were my family? The closer I got to Edgefield the more my excitement grew.

When I arrived at my cousin's house, I shared with him what I saw in the trees and what I thought they were, and he told me that I was right. He said they were old shacks, possibly slave quarters. He said that the trees grew over a lot of those old shacks. Ulysses was ready for me when I got there and he had it all planned out what we were going to do. He was going to take me to see everything. He took me to three different churches which, as I learned later in my research, played significant roles in my family's life: Bethel Bailey Baptist Church, Liberty Springs Baptist Church, and Springfield Missionary Baptist Church. Each church had a cemetery connected to it. I had family in all three. From my grandfather's 5-month old niece, Anna Jane Yeldell, being buried at Bailey Bethel, to my grandparents, great-grandparents, and even great-great-grandparents on my maternal grandmother's side, being buried in Springfield. I felt the spirit of my family no matter where I went.

Like anyone else who travels to a place with significance and meaning, I took lots of pictures, especially of headstones. The headstones gave me a sense of closure on my research. Each gave me proof of the ancestors' existence, and let me know that my research was well worth the brick walls and obstacles that I had overcome. The headstones let me know that I was finished with one portion of my search and that I could now move on to the next. After visiting the churches, I separated from Ulysses for a while to meet with the other people that were presenting during the Showcase. They were also newly found family members, who brought in more family names **(Bennet, Bush,** and **Butler)** and we were meeting in Edgefield to check-in and register for the conference. This would be my first time going into the city of Edgefield.

Driving into Edgefield was like traveling back in time. The ride was similar to the elevator ride in the New Smithsonian African American Museum. You would get on this elevator that was the size of a bedroom. As you went down on each side of the elevator was counting the years backward in time. When you got to the bottom you were in the 15th century. My ride to Edgefield was similar to that and by the time I got to the square I felt like I was in the 19th century. I had seen a picture of Edgefield during that time and not much had changed. The occupants of the stores may have changed, but I was willing to bet they were the same buildings in the picture. As a matter of fact, the biggest change was probably the fact that the streets were now paved. It was awesome and kind of spooky at the same time.

We all registered for the conference and then began our research. Just like the tombstones created closure for certain things, so did the paperwork that I found to attach to my earlier research. Once we finished, two of my newly found cousins,

Sheila and Gail, who was also related to my cousin Ulysses, wanted to meet him. We made our way back to Ulysses and he took us to the next stop on his agenda for me. The house that my maternal grandmother's mother lived.

Going to my maternal great-grandmother's house was an amazing experience and a story in itself. We had to go straight into those trees I spoke about on Highway 25. Was it a coincidence that the very thing that caught my attention while driving to Ulysses was one of the places I would end up going to see? I didn't think so. Researching was definitely teaching me to believe that nothing was a coincidence. There was an opening between two rows of trees. That opening was barely visible from the road, but it was the opening to a driveway that was over-grown with grass. As we drove down this driveway, I realized this was the path my mother had taken as a child when she visited with her mom over 65 years ago. Only she didn't have to ride with the windows rolled up.

The branches, filled with huge thick spider webs, were now wild and were beating the windows. The grass had grown so high that it reached halfway up the car. When we finally stopped, we were in an opening. Ulysses didn't know where the house was, and he wanted to be sure we didn't go too far or we would be at the top of a mountain. He looked to the left and said, "There it is." I was in total amazement. The pictures are of the home and barn of my mother's maternal grandparents, Lula and Johnnie Senior.

Figure 15 - Mama Lula's House, Photo taken by Donya Williams

The one time that I thought I should or could have cried, I wouldn't. But here I was, standing on the grounds where my grandmother grew up; the place that my mother used to come and visit. Looking at that porch every story that was ever recited to me became a

Figure 16 - Mama Lula's Barn, Photo taken by Donya Williams

reality. From my mother telling me how she sat and played with her cousin Ginny B., on the porch, to the picture of Mama Lula sitting in a rocking chair holding a pipe in her hand; I saw it all happening. I saw it all as if it was happening right in front of me. It was amazing! Going to Edgefield was becoming more than I had imagined. The possibility of meeting people who may have known my loved ones had come to pass and the spiritual connection I was receiving was overwhelming. Traveling to my great-grandmother's house, I wanted to kick into her research. So, I started my search on Mama Lula Peterson Senior, the mother of Annie Mae Senior-Yeldell.

"Mama Lula" Peterson-Senior

It would have been remiss of me not to try and find someone who may have known my family. The eldest members of my family who had been born in Edgefield were so very old, I knew that I probably wouldn't be meeting people of their generation. The likelihood was that I would be meeting the children of these people. The only person that seemed to have known anyone in my family was my cousin Ulysses. He remembered my grandfather, but not my grandmother. This made some sense since granddaddy Jeff was his great uncle. Ulysses is months younger than my mom, so what he remembered would be limited.

However, when I would ask other people about Lula Senior, everyone seemed to know who I was talking about. It seemed that, just like my grandparents, Mama Lula, her husband Papa Johnnie, their daughter (grandma Annie's sister) Essie, and their grandson, Eddie Senior, made a significant impact on the community. Even to this day, just the mention of their names draws recognition from the people I speak with. This definitely reminded me of the recognition the Yeldell name had at home in DC.

I was living up to my family's fame as well because of my research. With all of the cold calls I had made to Edgefield, my name preceded me, and people knew who I was. I spoke with one cousin by the name of James Ryans before my travels to Edgefield. James is my cousin in two ways. His great-grandmother, Alice Senior **Holloway**, was my great-grandfather Johnnie's sister and his uncle on his father's side, Willie Buster **Ryans**, married my grandmother's sister, Essie Senior Kemp Ryans. It was imperative that we got together to learn about our family. We decided to meet at the Tompkins Library. The story that I am about to share is on the day we were supposed to meet.

When I first got to Edgefield, I learned early on that cell phones did not work in certain areas. Contacting people would be a problem. The day that I was supposed to meet James at the library, I was in was of those bad connection areas and had no other way to contact him. Since I had no way of reaching him, I went to Springfield Baptist to take pictures of headstones. While snapping pictures, I heard my name called. I looked around and was a little frightened given the fact that my name was being called in a cemetery, and no one was around. I looked around and eventually just brushed it off and continued to take pictures, until I heard my name again.

I realized that people knew of me because of my constant cold calls and articles placed in the Edgefield Advertiser about my family. However, they didn't know what I looked like. Besides, this was in the middle of a cemetery in a state where very few people knew me by sight. This time I looked up and said, "Okay, look now stop playing, I have gotten used to my ancestors to a certain level, but I will still run." At that point, I turned around to face the church and this time I saw a man and a woman standing at the front of the cemetery. I walked over to them, assuming they were the ones that called my name and said, "Hello." The man introduced himself to me as my cousin James.

I couldn't believe it. I explained how I was not able to call him because of no service in the area. He explained to me that he realized that, so he decided to come to Springfield to visit the cemetery. I expressed to him that I was glad that he did, but I asked, "how did you know that was me standing way over there?" He replied, "I didn't." For some, they would just chalk this up to coincidence, but fellow researchers would only describe it as the ancestors getting involved and I tend to agree with them.

Meeting James the way I did was destiny because he handed me two pictures of family that I had never seen before. One was a lady named Joyce **Lagroon**. Joyce was the daughter of my great-grandfather's sister, Alice Senior Holloway, and the other picture was of Alice. Her picture was the only picture my mom and her siblings had of someone on their maternal grandfather's side of the family. I was forever grateful to my cousin James.

The trip to Edgefield was enlightening and extremely spiritual. I met several new family members who provided me with even more new surnames to research, and new phone numbers. Adding my maternal grandfather's grandparents' surnames to the list gave me **Holloways** and **Adams**. What's funny is the Holloways were added twice over because of a great Aunt marrying into the Holloway family. And if you are thinking to yourself 'was it the same family? That answer would be yes. Visiting Edgefield kept my research incentives high. My goal was to pull my family together one family line at a time. I left there with an even more determined spirit than before. My focus, when I returned home, was to take the information that I learned and search for my Peterson line.

My Petersons started with Mama Lula. Looking at her picture, I saw a petite woman who everyone was probably afraid of, and had nothing but respect for. She did not look as if she was someone you would misbehave with. If you look closely at the picture, you see a weird shaped object in her hand. That object was the pipe that my mother said Mama Lula smoked. My mother said although she was a little girl at the time, that she thought there was also a spittoon. With all that she did, I knew researching Mama Lula would definitely be something exciting.

Figure 17 - Lula "Mama Lula" Peterson-Senior, Photo
Courtesy of Juanita Yeldell-Williams

Chapter 7 – The Petersons

My search for Mama Lula was well anticipated. During the course of my research, the Petersons of Edgefield began appearing in different parts of my family tree within my mother's family. By the time I had made my trip to Edgefield, the Peterson family seemed to be everywhere in my mother's family. Every online search I did for one family line, that search would always end up connecting to the Petersons. I had to know more. I never understood why this happened. I just assumed they were a big family who had a large number of people who married into many of the other families of Edgefield.

I began my search and had found Mama Lula as a married woman with children just like I did her daughter. She was married to my Great Grandfather Papa Johnnie Senior on the 1900 U.S. Federal Census Records. There was no record of her however as a child, which meant I would not be able to learn who my grandparents were. The South Carolina Death Records were no help because the year she died was not available for viewing. This meant I was stuck, for the time being, that is until I received a message in my Ancestry.com mailbox from a man named Robert Palmore from Philadelphia. He explained to me that his cousin had connections with Lula Peterson (my maternal grandmother's mother) and that she had told him that Lula's father's name was Enoch Peterson. So, I gave him my number to give to her. Tonya Villa is the great-great-granddaughter of Enoch Peterson.

Tonya called me. Her mother listened to our conversation in the background. I was told that Tonya's grandmother had sat her mother down before she died and passed on all that she knew about the Peterson family. I don't remember Tonya's mother's name or which Peterson child they descended from, but she said, my great-grandmother, affectionately called Mama Lula's real name was Hazeltine Peterson. Hazeltine, as it would transpire, had been one of thirteen children. I was speechless and really tried to take this in. I asked my mother if she knew anything about the name Hazeltine for her grandmother and she didn't have a clue. As I thought about it, a different name could definitely explain why I couldn't find her as a child. Tonya had shared some very useful information, and I was eager to look into it. I went straight to my laptop and started to research my great-grandmother's possible father, Enoch Peterson.

I found Enoch Peterson married to a lady named Ann, and they did indeed have 13 children. Their names were: Enoch Jr., Goode, Joshua, Lottie, Hattie, Margaret, Oscar Joseph, Buelah, Lizzie, Mary and Dora (who were twins), Eliza, and finally, Carra. Hattie, according to Tonya, was supposed to be my great-grandmother, Mama Lula. I found her as a little girl living with Enoch Sr., and his wife Ann Shepherd in both the 1870 and the 1880 U.S. Federal Census. She went from Hazeltine in 1870 to Hattie in 1880. The one constant was her birth year. It never changed. Familiar with how the census records worked, I thought it possible that Hazeltine/Hattie was my maternal great-grandmother's first name.

The picture of her which I have shared in this book gives an impression of Mama Lula's inner strength and fortitude. She strikes me as a plain-speaking, 'I don't take any mess' type of woman. It wouldn't be a bad guess to say that she preferred the name Lula over Hazeltine/Hattie. Why she would prefer it remained, however, a mystery. Nevertheless, I felt certain that I had found my great-grandmother as a child.

I went for years thinking I knew who Mama Lula's parents were since the information I was given all seemed to fit. Using the traditional genealogical research methods, I found her siblings and as many of her sibling's children as possible. I discovered the Petersons were more than a family. They were their own tribe! Enoch had one son who had married twice and, between those two marriages, he had sixteen children. The number of ancestral Petersons that I was finding was astronomical. It actually started to scare me. There were so many that I made the decision to stop looking for them. There were simply too many new avenues of research to follow due to the sheer size of this family. Instead, I opted to focus on retrieving my great-grandmother's death certificate in order to solidify the information I had found for her.

Since it was not available online yet, I decided to order it. I thought my world would come to an end when I received her death certificate in the mail. Her death certificate stated that Lula's parents were Charles Peterson and Mollie Settles; and not Enoch and Ann! My first thought was this can't be right? All of the information that I found fit perfect. I couldn't deny it because the informant on the death certificate was my grandmother's sister, Essie. My next, and only, question was: who were Charles Peterson and Mollie **Settles**?

However, my second thought was more frightening than my first, because I thought to myself... OH MY GOD, my research is ruined! I had added hundreds of Petersons to my family tree that were not my family. What was I going to do? And, oh lord, I have to fix this. I started to research this new set of parents to see how well did they fit and how I could have been so wrong. My great-grandmother's real parents were Charles and Mollie Settles Peterson. There were some things that needed to be cleared up. First, I had to understand why it seemed Mama Lula had appeared with Enoch Peterson and Ann in the 1870 census, and second, I needed to determine if there was a family connection between her, Enoch, and Ann.

The Real Parents of Mama Lula Peterson Senior

Charles and Mollie Peterson did not have as many children as Enoch and Ann. In 1870, Enoch and Ann had six children, while Charles and Mollie had two. However, by 1880, Charles and Mollie had nine children. Their names were: Susie (**Holloway**), Ann (who was probably Mama Lula Senior), John, Fannie (1st m. **Carthen**, 2nd m. **Peterson**), Ella (**Williams**), Wesley, Alice, Mary, and Butler. I was unable to find Charles and Mollie after the 1880 Census. What I did find was the one thing that the two sets of parents had in common, and that was two little girls who were born at the same time. One was named Hazeltine and the other was named Ann. As a matter of fact, both Ann and Hazeltine were the only child within each respective household whose birth year never changed in the census records. I could now see why the two had confused me.

I was satisfied with the information the death certificate provided until I was contacted by a woman, who will remain nameless, who would try to again change everything. She said that the young Ann, who lived with Charles and Mollie was not my great-grandmother, but another woman who would have been Mama Lula's sister. Ann, the woman that I found to be my great-grandmother, according to her, was really Fannie. It appeared the census taker had written her name down incorrectly.

When I told her that the death certificate for Mama Lula stated that Charles Peterson and Mollie Settles-Peterson were her parents, this woman was quick to say that the information was wrong. I explained to the lady that my great-grandmother's daughter was the informant, so she would know who her grandparents were. The lady insisted that the information was incorrect. I was confused and simply didn't know what to think or what to believe. Did I believe what the vital records stated? Or trust the word of a well-intentioned family member?

I started to think to myself, okay Donya, the death certificate is only as reliable as the person giving the information, and when I asked about my grandfather's parents, Aunt Lula wasn't sure of her grandparent's name so maybe the lady is right maybe the informant on Mama Lula's death certificate didn't know the names of her grandparents either? The only problem I had with this was, this wasn't just any informant, this was Mama Lula's daughter Essie. Listening to my mom, Aunt Essie was the gatekeeper to our history. How could she be wrong?

There was a post making the rounds on Facebook. It was one of those memes that are popularly shared on social media. It was a picture of a bench with accompanying text that posed a simple question: if there was anyone you could choose to talk to on this bench who would it be? My answer would have been Aunt Essie. I thought about it some more and remembered when my Aunt Lula had said she wasn't certain about the names of her grandparents but she ended up being correct. There had to be some other way to prove the death certificate and the information provided by my grandmother's sister was correct. The 1890 census was destroyed, so that wouldn't be a resource I could use. The death certificate seemed to be my only reliable source. This was a doozy. I went to my fellow genealogist/family members.

One of my cousins is a genius with checking old newspapers. She was able to find several obituaries for our family. I asked her if she could find one for Mama Lula. Why look for an obituary? When researching, it's best to think outside of the box. You should check things that, in most instances, wouldn't be obvious. Most obituaries give information about the names of parents, the names of any children, the married names of daughters, if any had married, the names of siblings, as well as the names of the towns, cities, counties and states where surviving family members were living at the time of that person's death. An obituary for Mama Lula, if one even existed, could provide any of this information. This information could, in turn, provide more proof of who her parents were.

I am sure you are asking "What do you mean if one existed? An obituary in the paper for African Americans did not become common until around the 1930s. This is not to say that there were not write-ups in the papers about African Americans, but just not like this. However, she didn't find an obituary for Mama Lula, but she did find them for several of her siblings. Each obituary listed my great-grandmother as their sister, including Fannie's obituary.

Fannie, if you recall, was listed in the 1870 Census as the young Ann Peterson. I also ordered the death certificate for Fannie. When that document arrived, I learned that Fannie was not born at the same time as Mama Lula, nor did she have Ann in her name. I proved it. Mama Lula was Ann, and Fannie was her sister. I was satisfied.

Just like the first set of Petersons I thought were connected to Mama Lula, I began to do it again. This time adding the correct siblings and their children that were connected to her through Charles and Mollie and just like the first set of Petersons, this new family line grew exponentially. Of what I found, five of Charles and Mollie's eight children had produced forty-three grandchildren, and an ocean liner passenger load of great-grandchildren. As I continued my search of Charles and Mollie Peterson children more descendants revealed themselves. Each of Charles and Mollie's children had gone on to have produced children numbering in the double digits.

It was similar, if not exactly, like entering the information that I had done previously for Enoch and Ann Peterson. Could the very act of producing such a large number of children, all born at regular intervals, be a clue in and of itself to a possible relationship between these two Peterson family lines? Let's look at this from a different angle. If red hair, or freckles, or blue eyes are passed down family lines... could the same be true for reproductive traits? Could a genealogist even use such a factor to determine a family relationship? And was this something unique to the Petersons? Was it a trait I could document in the family lines that the Petersons' married into? Or was it something that was unique to Edgefield? And if so, why? Was this a trait that was pronounced among my ancestral black family lines in Edgefield – or would I also see the same biological dynamic in the white families I knew I was related to in Edgefield? There were many questions to answer.

As always, once I finish my search of my direct relative I begin to look at their siblings. I started with Mama Lula's sister Fannie. She married a man named Enoch Peterson Jr. Now to cut right to it, he was the son of Enoch and Ann Peterson, the first set of Petersons I originally had as Mama Lula's parents. Finding this information, I went deeper into Enoch Jr's story and learned he was married once before to a woman named Jane Stephens. The sixteen children that I had found were the children of two women, and not one. Of course, I was ready to stop. I had already experienced one brush at entering this family's information on my family tree. It scared me then and it was scaring me now, especially when I saw that my own Peterson family wasn't exactly small. I just made sure I stuck with my maternal great-grandparents' family only. I was content with my approach and focused specifically on Mama Lula's children.

Now, remember when I told you that to talk about my grandmother's siblings, I had to wait until I got to a certain area? Well, this was that area. For a quick recap, my grandmother was Annie Mae Senior Yeldell and she was one of ten children. Of those ten children, five of them had given Charles and Mollie over twenty-three great-grandchildren. My grandmother Annie, their granddaughter, had given them the most with thirteen, and another of their daughters, my Aunt Essie, came second with seven children.

While entering Aunt Essie's children to the tree, an oral story that I had been told was proven. This story was originally about the Yeldells being related to the **Harrison** family. Well, if you remember Mary Palmore was married to my grandfather's brother Gary Yeldell and with him, he had four children. When Gary died Mary remarried into the Harrison family making this her second marriage. Since the story of Harrison's and Yeldell's was one that I had to prove entering her children with the Harrison marriage gave the proof of relation. However, another connection to the Harrison family emerged while entering the children of my grandmother's sister Essie's children. It was this find, alongside many others, that gave me the title of this book.

My First Encounter with Double Cousins

Preparing your mind for genealogy research is mandatory. If you don't, you will have reactions like Ben Affleck did when he learned his family owned slaves. You are either going to be okay with what you find, or you will not. If you are not okay with it, then you shouldn't research. It is that simple. But if you decide that you want to know something, regardless of what you may find it really is mandatory that you get yourself ready for whatever you are going to come across. For instance, it still bothers me to this day that my nineteen-year-old grandfather, Jefferson Yeldell, was courting my fourteen-year-old grandmother, Annie Mae Senior. In this day and age that would be classed as statutory rape. If Annie Mae had been my child, he either would have been in jail or I would have been for using the men in the family to chase him off. However, I have to remind myself of context.

The context, in this case, was the social norms of the day. But back then, travel was limited, and so was the number of people within the rural communities dotted throughout Edgefield. Remember, Edgefield was a very rural and seemed to be a very isolated part of South Carolina. In the time period when Annie Mae and Jefferson lived, if a woman made it to the age of twenty without being married, she was considered to be a spinster or old maid. There weren't any career options available for single women; not in Edgefield, and certainly not for women of color, much less women of color who were poor. You either married or kept house for a parent or unmarried brother. So, for the times, my grandparent's marriage was acceptable.

Edgefield was a small town and travel was limited. I had found two incredibly large Peterson family lines. The children from those lines had to marry someone. If travel was a barrier to marrying someone from outside of their community, they had to marry people from within their community. I was beginning to sense that the people my Edgefield relations were marrying, were cousins. I'll put it in the following way. It dawned on me that in a community such as Edgefield, you were faced with three choices if you were going to tie the knot. The first choice was accepting the fact that you were going to be marrying a cousin of some description. The second choice was not marrying at all, which went against the social norms of the times. Or, thirdly, you had to leave the area. This last option posed significant implications.

Leaving the area meant leaving everyone and everything you'd ever know behind. It meant abandoning the one bedrock of support any person can have – your family. You would need to find a job, most likely without references because no one in a new town or city would know who you were. You would also find a place to live. The challenges would be significant, especially if you were a person of color in a period of time when Jim Crow laws were beginning to really bite. Added to this, there weren't any certainties that you would find a marriage partner even if you should choose to leave. Understanding all of this, cousin marriages disturbed me. Although I understood the whys and hows of how these marriages came to be, it didn't make it any easier when I found evidence of them. It is for this reason that I want to share with you my first encounter with double cousins, and how I reacted.

As I stated earlier, this discovery first happened while entering my Aunt Essie's children into my tree. While entering information on Essie's family, her daughter's husband John Jr. name kept popping up. This is another instance of how the more you enter people into your tree, the more the process begins to help you. I realized, however, that his name continued to re-occur because the name I was entering was already in my tree. John Jr. was the son of uncle Gary's Yeldell's widow, Mary Palmore Yeldell Harrison. John Jr. was her son by her second husband, John Harrison. While updating the information for this family in my tree, I found that Mary's second husband John Sr. was the son of Phillip Harrison and Agnes Senior.

Agnes was my great-grandfather Johnnie Senior's sister, which made Agnes Mama Lula's sister-in-law. If you don't see it yet this made Aunt Essie's daughter a first-cousin-once-removed with her husband. Originally, I was mortified. It was harder for me to wrap my head around this when I found out that my maternal 2nd great-grandmother, Martha, was a breeder. It wasn't because it was family marrying family. I mean, that really got to me, but the fact that I may have to tell my cousin that his mom and dad were related frightened me even more.

A friend of mine directed me to a website about these types of relationships, and what I learned was amazing. It seems there are state laws regarding marriage between first cousins. It states,

"Twenty-five states prohibit marriages between first cousins. Six states allow first cousin marriage under certain circumstances, and North Carolina allows first cousin marriage but prohibits double-cousin marriage. States generally recognize marriages of first cousins married in a state where such marriages are legal[45]." However, what got me the most was this last sentence "This page was last updated on May 2010 and will no longer be updated moving forward." The fact that the last time this page was updated was seven years ago made my jaw drop. It was confirmed that it was time for me to get over this. America did and so should I.

When I shared my findings with my cousin's wife, I was glad to learn that he was aware of this family connection. As I continued my research, I found more and more evidence of cousin marriages within my Edgefield family. The surnames that were intermarrying came from all over Edgefield. My search began with just two names, and now I was directly connected to eight different surnames. I had only reached the 2x great-grandparent level in my research. Already I was discovering that all of these families were connected to one another. In a very real way, they were all part of the same family; a very large family with numerous surnames.

Those names were Adams, Brooks, Holloway, Peterson, Senior, Settles, Williams, and Yeldell. This didn't include our extended cousins like Addison, Fisher, Freeman, Harrisons, Jones, Palmore, Peterson and Ryans. The surname count of my relatives included at least 30 families. What had I gotten myself into? I continued my search and found another connection to the first set of Petersons, that would-be Enoch Peterson's line. I learned that Enoch's grandson, Bishop married one of my great-grandfather's Papa Johnnie's nieces.

Why was this family showing up again? I have researched long enough to know that this wasn't a coincidence. So instead of ignoring the obvious, I went on ahead and re-entered Enoch Peterson Sr. and his family. As I entered the info that I had, I ended up finding more of the same name Edgefield surnames among the marriages. It had become ridiculous and I was starting to believe that all of Edgefield were related.

I had to cut back on the family tree building because I just couldn't take constantly finding double cousins. I took a break to learn more about Enoch Sr., and, in the process, found that he did something extraordinary. He was an agriculturist in Edgefield, one who seemed to have been respected enough that when he died, there was a write-up about him in a paper. I was unable to find exactly where the article was written but was able to capture a picture of it. It was something close to an obituary; very unusual during that time for a black man.

After reading more of the article, I realized it was more about what he died from than the fact that he actually died. It explained that Enoch died in 1909 from pellagra - a niacin deficiency disease caused by improper diet, and characterized by skin lesions, gastrointestinal disturbances, and nervousness. Depression, dermatitis, dementia, and diarrhea are common symptoms.

Three million Americans contracted pellagra and 100,000 died of it from 1906-40.[46] This disease was a huge problem for the poor specifically the enslaved in the south for that lack of a proper diet. They were always given the scraps of what was left so they had to make do with that. According to medicinenet.com the meals for the poor in the south consisted of the "three M's": meat (pork fatback); molasses; and meal (cornmeal).[47]

That wasn't all I found about Enoch. I had come across a contract that made him an indentured slave. I didn't realize it until my cousin Gail pointed out that she had never heard the term indentured slave before. We had both heard of indentured servant, but I couldn't say for sure if I had heard of an indentured slave. This was definitely worth looking into.

Enoch Peterson – The Indentured Slave

I got the term indentured slave from the document that I uncovered, which read that he gave up his freedom. The contract dated 1867 shows that Enoch would be an indentured slave until the land he wanted to buy was purchased. The land he purchased was on the Major Bowles property. I thought to myself, why would he voluntarily become an indentured slave for a piece of land? I needed to learn the difference between the two terms which caused me to go into more research about the term Indentured servant.

The first thing I did was look up the meaning of indentured slave. I didn't find anything for that specific term, but I did find a definition or explanation for what an indentured servant was. Indentured servitude "is a system whereby young people paid for their passage to the New World by working for an employer for a certain number of years. It was widely employed in the 18th century in the British colonies in North America and elsewhere"[48]. This definition, however, just didn't seem to apply to this particular person. I did a little more research and found a website about a PBS show called History Detectives Special Investigations. This show went into a little more detail on how indentured servitude worked.

Servants typically worked for four to seven years in exchange for passage, room, board, lodging and freedom dues[49] (basically what the definition said). While the life of an indentured servant was harsh and restrictive, it wasn't slavery. In 1619, the first black Africans came to Virginia. With no slave laws in place, they were initially treated as indentured servants and given the same opportunities for freedom dues as whites. However, slave laws were soon passed—in Massachusetts in 1641 and Virginia in 1661—and any small freedoms that might have existed for blacks were taken away[50].

Now that I understood the meaning of an indentured servant, it was my guess that Enoch Sr., may have been a free man of color, and what could pass as a standard indentured service contract had been adapted for this specific set of circumstances. They couldn't call him an indentured servant because the rules for an indentured servant did not apply to black people. Enoch must have had proof of being free, and he was not going to give that up. The contract was written that he would work as an indentured slave until the land was paid for. The guess was a long shot, but it was the only thing that made sense.

I wanted to know what was so important about this land that he would sacrifice his freedom, even for a limited amount of time in, order to own it. This was new territory for me. Researching land and property records was not something that I had done before. I went to a fellow researcher and family member, Natonne, to tell her what I found. She proceeded to explain to me that one of the churches I spoke about earlier could be the land he was trying to purchase. She stated that she had the deed to Springfield Missionary Baptist Church of Edgefield. On that deed was listed the names of the founders of the church. There were five founders: Joshua Peterson, Andrew **Harrison**, Pickens **Rearden**, Miles Holloway and the Reverend Ned **Starks**.

Again, we have the surnames Peterson, Holloway, and Harrison. Stark was the person who initiated the establishment of the church, which involved the four other men. Stark was the first pastor. I went back and looked at the contract Enoch signed and found the name of the land and where it was located. The Springfield Missionary Baptist church was in this same location. Enoch had made himself an indentured slave to purchase the land that the church still sits on to this day. How awesome was that!

This, however, still didn't explain what his motivation was. I then looked at the founders, and the name Joshua Peterson kind of leaped out at me. My first thought was, could Joshua and Enoch be related? Did Enoch buy the land to help Joshua and the other founders? Several other questions popped into my head as well. Since this was the church my family attended, could Joshua be the reason why they attended this church? Is there a relationship between my great-grandmother's Peterson line and Joshua? Could all three of the Peterson men I have found so far be connected? I was now made to dig deep into the Peterson history to try to find these connections.

Once I realized what I had to do, I was totally upset. I had to dig into the same family that had scared me off researching them. I was dreading this search for several reasons, but the two most important were 1) because of the size of the Peterson family, and 2) my search for them would start from the early to mid-1800s. It is hard to search from that time period for many genealogists. For African Americans, it's incredibly challenging due to the lack of traditional records for enslaved people. I had to try. I wasn't quite sure how this was all connecting with me, but I could feel it in my bones that it was.

I went back to Mama Lula's family and looked at her parents (the biological ones). I went to the 1870 census and, at the very top of it, were my 2nd great-grandparents, Charles and Mary (a.k.a. Mollie) Peterson with their two oldest daughters, one of which is my great-grandmother Mama Lula (a.k.a. Ann). I started to look at the families who lived in the neighborhood and learned there were several sets of Petersons living on the same block, along with my 2nd great-grandparents. There were William and Caroline Peterson, Wiley and Sally Peterson, and a Hannah Peterson with her family. What I found even more interesting was an older, Peterson couple named Peter and Violet, who was living in the center of all of these Petersons.

I learned early in my research that family members tend to live close to each other. It was an educated guess that the elderly couple I had found, Peter and Violet Peterson, were, in fact, the parents of the other Petersons living on that block. That educated guess was all that I had. The adults on that block were born in the early to mid-1800s—slavery times—so searching their names in pre-1870 census records were useless. I went years, hitting dead-end after dead-end in trying to prove my theory. Then, one day, I traveled back to Edgefield for Springfield's 145th church anniversary. It was here that I received the break of a lifetime.

I had my mom's DNA tested and learned of several new cousins. One of whom was a man named Gary Myles. While the DNA showed that Gary was my mom's cousin, none of us knew how, or who the common while in Edgefield, Gary connected me to his mom via telephone conversation, who in turn connected, me to her dad over the phone as well. Her dad knew the names of the Petersons I was researching! He even had a written history that gave the names of all the Petersons who were related. This history said, "Our family began with a man who was named Peter Bangley and lived in Wheeling, West Virginia. During the course of time, his name became Peterson. Peter was married to an Indian lady and to that union they had nine (9) children: Charles, Wiley, Daniel, George Washington (Big Watt), Enoch (Big), Amanda, Georgeanna, and Anna."

It seemed my educated guess was correct. Peter and Violet were my 3rd great-grandparents! I looked at the census record again and saw that Amanda and Georgeanna also lived on the same street. As I continued to view the entire census for Edgefield for that year, Daniel and Enoch followed one and two pages later. Learning this let me know that Enoch Peterson belonged on my tree after all; not as my 2nd great-grandfather, but as my 2nd great-granduncle. It also pointed out that Fannie Peterson, Mama Lula's sister, married her first cousin Enoch Jr. I told you I needed to get over that quickly because it was obvious that this was just the beginning. Getting the information from Gary's grandfather brought my Petersons line to the fore.

I was meeting descendant after descendant; from my 2x great-grandfather's siblings. I had met descendants of Enoch, Daniel, Wiley, and Amanda's families four out of the thirteen children. It was starting to look like every Peterson from the Edgefield County area was related. I had not connected Joshua Peterson directly, but several of the DNA cousins that matched my mom was connected to him. We didn't know the link, but I am pretty positive the connection is through him. It also started to look like the Petersons were the family that connected me to other families throughout the Edgefield area. Most importantly, I found they didn't have a problem marrying and having children with each other. This meant uncovering more instances of double cousins by the hundreds, and hours deciphering what I was seeing in my tree. But this time it was worth it because another brick wall had been knocked down.

The Peterson line was amazing. They were a large family who didn't seem to have come from enslavement. As an African-American researcher, you automatically assume that your surname comes from the last family that "owned" your newly freed ancestors. However, my research proved that my Petersons had actually been enslaved in the neighboring Newberry County, South Carolina before ending up in Edgefield. While their enslavement, at this point, seems to have been associated with the Petersons in Newberry, they were owned by a different family in Edgefield.

I learned my Peterson family experience was the opposite of

Martha Brooks. Martha and most of her children had been held within the same family until liberated through the Emancipation Proclamation. The Petersons, however, had been split apart between different families during the course of slavery. This made me realize that finding them living on the same block in 1870 was more than just luck. Although they were separated between Newberry and Edgefield, they ended up back together as a family in the end. The more I researched, the more they connected me to other families in Edgefield. We were connected as cousins to **Burtons, Gilchrist, Holloways (same family), Lewis, Matthews, Rabbs and Settles (same family)**. I pulled back on my research on the Peterson's and started to work on Mama Lula's husband, Papa Johnnie Senior. I needed to see who they connected us to as well.

Figure 18 - Senior Family Women, Photos courtesy of James Ryan and Juanita Yeldell-Williams, Collage by Donya Williams

Chapter 8 – The Senior Family

My research for my great-grandfather, Johnnie Senior a.k.a. Papa Johnnie was straightforward. This was a blessing coming out of researching other complicated family lines. Johnnie was the son of Johnnie and Jane Senior. He was the seventh child out of ten. The names of Johnnie and Jane's children were: Versey, Alice, Agnes, Anna, Moses, Henderson, Johnnie (Papa Johnnie), Job, Elvira, and Jane. I was told by my mother that Papa Johnnie was a full-blooded Cherokee Indian.

During the mid to late 1870s the Federal Government recognized only five tribes: Cherokee, Choctaw, Muscogee (Creek), Chickasaw, and Seminole who was a group of Native American nations that the term was applied by Anglo-European settlers during the colonial and early federal period because these tribes had adopted many of the colonists' customs and generally, had good relations with the white settlers. If I were to learn more about a Native American connection, I would have to access a completely different set of genealogical records pertaining specifically to Native Americans from the East Coast and Mississippi River Valley region. So, when I started to call around it seemed I needed to prove that I personally was of Native American heritage before I could get into those records. I was confused because I needed those records to prove my Native American Heritage. I was in a catch twenty-two.

My cousin Sheila had introduced me to a Native American chief and he tried to explain to me how to start researching my Native American heritage. He gave me quite a bit to read. It was so much reading that I realized this research was something totally different. The time devoted to this would take me in a different direction from what I was doing. I didn't want to stop the roll I was on, but I promised both him and myself that I would come back to it.

The Siblings of Johnnie Senior

When it came to my great-grandfather, Johnnie Senior a.k.a. Papa Johnnie, although the first part of my search for him seemed easy (since I already found him with his wife Mama Lula Peterson) searching for his parents and the rest of his siblings proved to be extremely difficult. Their parents, John and Jane Williams-Senior seemed to have just appeared in the Edgefield area right before the 1870 census and disappeared after the 1880 census was taken. I also noticed that anyone who carried the name Senior as a surname seemed to have been my immediate family in Edgefield. However, in its surrounding counties, I didn't know who they were and they didn't seem to connect to us. They appeared and disappeared, however, just like my great-grandparents.

I tried finding a possible slaveholding family, but there were no Caucasian people with the surname Senior in Edgefield or anywhere even close to it. As a matter of fact, the only Caucasian people who carried Senior as a surname lived in England. So, I didn't know how they got their names, if they were once enslaved or where they even came from. Despite the difficulty, I continued the search for more of my great-grandfather's siblings and their children.

Out of his ten siblings, I was only able to find his sister Alice, who married John **Holloway (same family),** his sister Agnes, who married Phillip **Harrison (same family)**, his sister Elvira, who married Lawton **Moore,** and his brother Moses who married Lila **Fisher (same family)**. Each family had, at one point or the other, looped back into the overall family. As I spoke with other members who knew about the inbreeding, they didn't understand why these stories were kept secret. To me, it was a lot to take in. However, I understood at least why it was happening during this time period.

When I spoke with one cousin connected to the Harrison line, he asked me, "Why are you doing this?" My answer was simple "Our family doesn't know each other. If we don't know each other, we are prone to repeat the same things." When I said that he shared with me that all of the Harrisons in the Edgefield area were related. And not just Edgefield, Harrisons from the surrounding counties, were family as well. This meant we may have shared a connection to the Andrew Harrison, who was one of the founders of Springfield Baptist, the church Enoch Peterson, Sr., was associated with. The land this church sat upon had been acquired through Enoch's brief time as an indentured slave.

My Edgefield surname connection now stood at forty-five names. These were not distant cousins. As a matter of fact, no one was beyond being my third cousin. The more I searched, the more surnames I found. Eventually, I stopped researching Papa Johnnie siblings and instead, I tried to see what I could discover about his parents. My thought was that if I searched for his parents, this avenue of research might indirectly help me find more of his siblings. Researching his parents was even more difficult than attempting to locate Johnnie's missing siblings. His parents were born between the 1790s and the very early. This meant I had to search internationally, and I just wasn't monetarily ready for an international search. I tried my luck with his wife Jane.

Who is Jane Senior?

Genealogy is a mix of common sense, geometry, and biology. Let's look at the process of a woman from a baby until she gets married to better understand this theory. When women are born, they carry the surname of their father until they marry. That same surname or what we call our maiden until we marry changes to the husband's name. If she marries more than once, a woman's surname will change with each subsequent marriage. That part is common sense. The biology comes in with the educated guess or hypothesis, like when I had to guess about Enoch Sr. and the meaning of the Indentured Slave contract he signed. The geometry comes in with providing proof for the theorems. If you remember, the goal in geometry is to prove an angle was an angle, and what type of angle it could be.

With Jane, I ended up having to use all three skills. I found Jane and Papa Johnnie's father, John, in two instances: in the 1870 and 1880 U.S. Federal Census records. Both times, their children were living with them. Jane was having children seemingly the same way her granddaughter, (my grandmother) Annie Mae, had done: every eighteen months to two years. Since I knew Jane's maiden name from one of her child's death certificate, I decided to do a fresh search of Jane using her maiden name and her birth year.

When the information came back, of course, I found her in the 1870 and 1880 U.S. Federal Census records. I noticed, however, in the 1870 census that there was a woman named Jane Williams. My great grandmother was listed as Jane Senior but this other woman who was listed as Jane Williams stood out to me. This Jane lived in the Grey Township area of Edgefield while my Jane was in the Blocker township area of Edgefield – the distance between the two townships was 22 miles. I was drawn to this Jane Williams because her birth year was 1837, two years distant from my great grandmother Jane Senior. I was starting to feel like Jane Williams might also be my Jane Senior. I re-examined the two 1870 census records I had found, citing the two different Janes. I looked at the date each record was enumerated. The one for the woman I knew to be Jane Senior was taken 1 August 1870. The one for Jane Williams was taken on 20 August 1870. Could one person be counted twice?

Jane Williams was listed as living with an older couple, Moses and Eada Williams, along with her four children: Savannah, Andrew, Anna, and Walton. My educated guess, of course, led me to believe that the older couple was her parents. However, I found it odd that Savannah and Anna's birth years were very close to the two birth years given to my great-grandfather's sisters, Versey and May. I also found that the person my great grandfather's sister would end up marrying, lived a few doors down from Jane Williams parents, Moses and Eada Williams. This is important because family tends to live around other family members. I began to wonder what I had just stumbled upon. Could my Jane, Versey, and May Senior be the same mother and daughters of Jane, Savannah, and Anna Williams? Was this another coincidence, or were the ancestor's intervening again? Was Anna May Settles actually Jane Williams' daughter? If so, was Jane Williams one in the same as Jane Senior?

The best thing about my research was finding a family member that was willing to share information and help me with researching Jane. So many times, we find people who are researching the same family, ask you what you know but don't want to share what they know. It is important to share because sometimes you can be the key to knocking down a brick wall, or vice versa. My family and I work together as a team. When one of us needs to learn more about a particular family, we would refer them to another family member who had the most knowledge about that particular family.

For me, I turned to the researchers on the Settles line. The researchers for the Settles family had gone so deep into the Settles family history, it would have been ridiculous for me to try to go back and find the same information they already knew. Because of them, my European line on the Settles side had gone back in time well into the 17th century. We decided to focus on Jane and Anna because they were the two people these cousins knew the most about. They didn't think the two Jane's and Anna's were the same.

In their search, they had found Jane Williams to be a slave who was owned by William J. Harling. It is believed that Mr. Harling was, in fact, Anna's father. Which meant that Johnnie Senior, Sr., was not her father. There was more information they had and it was pretty convincing. Despite all I had was a gut feeling, I still felt like the two Jane's were one in the same, as well as the two Anna's. I just didn't have a leg to stand on at that moment.

My cousin Charles, who is a Settles researcher as well as a Yeldell researcher, told me the only way we could definitively prove that Jane and Anna Williams were the same people as Jane and Anna Senior was to have a DNA test. My mom had already done a DNA test. So that box was ticked from our side. We needed to find a match within her genetic cousins to see who matched her from the Settles side of the family tree. Mom shared DNA with one of my fellow genealogist's parents. It was her father who popped up as 2nd to 3rd cousin to my mom. It was at that point we discovered that Jane Williams-Senior was his great-grandmother. The same Jane Williams-Senior who was also the great-grandmother to my mom.

Additionally, another woman popped up on several of our Settles family DNA lists. These lists were names of people who had also taken the DNA test and popped up as a match/relative to my mother and other family members. We would compare our list to see if we shared matches. Birdie was on that compared list. When I checked, she shared DNA with my mom and a man whose username was Trezzy123. We learned that Trezzy123 was the grandson of one of Papa Johnnie's sibling because his mother Mary was a Senior who married into the **Trezevant** family. I was excited to learn this, but it also caused me to chuckle. If you caught the name Trezevant that Mary married into, it was also the last name of the man who dueled Preston Brooks. That name was as rare as Yeldell and like the Yeldell's if you shared the name you probably share the blood.

This was yet another great find. I had proved that Jane's parents Moses and Eada Williams were my 3rd great-grandparents. If I hadn't taken the chance of trying to find out more about Jane I would have never learned that she was listed twice on the 1870 census all because she was visiting her parents at the time the census was being taken. Since I had become so lucky in finding Jane I was going to take my chances on her parents.

Chapter 9 – Moses Williams

According to the newspaper USA Today, genealogy is the second most popular hobby in the U.S. Its popularity hit the media in 1997 through Brigham Young University. They produced a show called Ancestors that gave instructions on how to start researching your family history. Then again in 2006 with a show called African American Lives. This second show provided a view into the lives and family history of well-known African Americans. The show was upgraded in 2009 to include people of all nationalities, which brought about the name change to Faces of America. Both shows debuted on the PBS channel. It wasn't until 2010 that Lisa Kudrow adopted the popular British genealogy show, Who Do You Think You Are? for American audiences on NBC.

Who Do You Think You Are? led to an upswing in the general public's interest in discovering their own family's history. Finding Your Roots, with Henry Louis Gates, aired in 2016, keeping a focus on celebrities. As the various genealogy-related shows matured and progressed, the information they provided, specifically for African American research, was not that informative. In fact, I started to think I had either become too advanced or they were conducting searches for African Americans that were on an easier scale. Those shows made me lose interest.

The shows that have become more interesting to me were the shows featured on the Brigham Young University broadcast. These shows featured everyday people who I felt I could connect to on a personal level. I think every genealogist has a story or two that would make shows like Finding Your Roots or Who Do You Think You Are? drop to their knees. I know I had at least three in this book. The story of Moses was one of them. Now don't get me wrong, my family is an amazing group of people. However, the story of Moses was, without a doubt, the most unbelievable story a person could hear.

I thought I was just going to fall right into telling the story of Moses just like I did with the others. However, I realized that because he was born in the late 1790s, right after the first ever U.S. Federal Census, it was taking me into the 18th Century. This period of time went deeper into slavery than I had ever gone before. Explaining his story would be difficult. I wanted to make sure I didn't bore you, and this research would have me knee deep in probate records, slave sale deeds, and land deeds. I appreciate that these kinds of records could be uninteresting to some people. I knew this was going to be a lot more technical. However, this story is worth the challenge. For African Americans with enslaved ancestors, the methodology used to research Moses Williams is critical to understand. You will have to use the same research tools in researching your own enslaved ancestors.

Researching an ancestor during the 18th Century is difficult for any race of people in America. For example, from 1790 to 1840, the only named listed on the U.S. Federal census is the head of the house. Spouses and children are not listed or referenced by name. Any additional information is counted by the number of people in the house according to age. However, for African-Americans, things were different. Even though you were free you still had a guardian. There were some that had their own place and if they did, they were listed just like white people. But there were some who lived with their guardian and if they did then you didn't see their names. At that point, as an African American researcher, you would have to know who your family's guardian was.

But if your family were not free people of color, your difficulty of finding your ancestors increases to the point where it seems to be pretty much impossible. It is because of this difficulty coupled with the 1850 and 1860 slave schedules that list our families by age and gender only you hear the statement "my history was erased" or "it is impossible for me to find my family before the 1870 census." It's not impossible. I am living proof of that. Nevertheless, it is a challenge with all manner of barriers to slow your progress down.

Since he was born in the 1790s, I started my search for Moses in old newspaper articles. I did this because it was extremely doubtful that he would personally have a death certificate. When he died in South Carolina, it was decades before the mandate for death certificates. Of course, he could have been named on a death certificate of a child as a parent, but he wouldn't have had one for himself. Searching through newspaper articles for him, I was hoping he would be like my 2x great-uncle, Enoch Peterson, a farmer who was associated with something important enough to receive a mention in the paper.

Well, he did just that and although it had something to do with raising or taking care of something it had nothing to do with farming. I found an article called Quintuplets and More on the website Newspapers.com. The article discussed the topic of multiple births of children and families with large numbers of children. Within the article were subtitles citing different instances that had to do with specific groups of children. I came across this one:

Excerpt from "Quintuplets and More

Negro Farmer Had 45 Children

The fecundity of the Negro race has been the subject of much comment and discussion. A case has come to light in this state that is one of the most remarkable on record. Moses Williams, a negro farmer, lives in the eastern section of this State. He is sixty-five years old (as nearly as he can make out), but does not appear to be over fifty. He has been married twice, and by the two wives has had born to him 45 children. By the first wife he had 23 children, 20 of whom were girls and 3 were boys. By the second wife he had 22 children – 20 girls and 2 boys. He also has about 50 grandchildren. The case is well authenticated."[51]

Yeah, you read it right, forty-five children. This article was syndicated in several different papers around the United States, as well as published in a book of medical anomalies. Can you imagine how I felt when I read the article? It was six o'clock in the morning. And there I was learning that I might be the 3x great-granddaughter of a man who had forty-five children. To put it lightly, it was all a little overwhelming. But how did I know that he was my 3x great-grandfather? Well, the truth is I didn't know at the time. My first instinct, my genealogist's instinct, told me that he was. Once I let that instinct kick-in, I became sad. I knew that I now had to try and prove that my instinct was right. This meant that I was going to have to find as many of these unknown children as I could, and then prove they were related to me.

The sheer scale of the endeavor was depressing. In case you still don't understand why this made me so sad, take the information you have learned so far from reading this book and think: Who is harder to find, men or women? Now try to imagine looking for forty girls who were born long before, and even into, the Civil War Era, with last names that change with every marriage. I bet you see my dilemma now. I shared my findings with the different genealogical groups I am a part of on Facebook. You could immediately tell the difference between the new researchers and the more seasoned ones.

The newbies were excited and congratulatory while the seasoned ones started off with a laugh and said good luck. I called my cousin Sheila, who is definitely one of the seasoned researchers, and told her about my findings. She laughed so hard that a tear or two probably rolled down her cheek. She told me I made her day and that she really needed that laugh. My cousin Brian, however, kept the laughter in and instead showed as close to some sympathy as I was going to get from any researcher. He and Sheila both understood my pain because they knew as much as I was fussing, I was going to try to figure this out, and they knew what was ahead of me.

As I discussed this find with Brian, he hit me with something that hadn't even crossed my mind. He was the first person to point out that discovering Moses Williams had the potential to connect my father's side of the family to my mother's side of the family. At that point, I told him "Brian, I am not in the mood for this Williams family." He responded with "OKAY". But I knew what his "okay" really meant. While I was venting, Brian's mind was moving at warp speed, figuring out a plan of attack. While talking to me about the situation, he went and found another article. It said:

Obituary Notes

"Moses Williams colored aged 115 years died in Barnwell, S.C. yesterday. He was the father of forty-three children, all of whom are living – Charleston Courier."[52]

I was so overwhelmed with what had to be done that I just couldn't do it. He contacted me the next day with a plan of how we would find the children of Moses Williams. Brian took this as the Genealogy Gods setting him up for a challenge, and he accepted. Before I go any further, let me explain the relationship between Brian and me. Remember when I said the descendants of Peter and Violet were coming from everywhere?

Well, Brian is one of them. He is a DNA cousin that I found about five years ago, who shared a connection through Peter and Violet's daughter, Amanda. Since that time, we have learned that we are cousins through five different lines, which means we share at least five sets of common ancestors, and Moses Williams was one of them. I knew that he was going to jump into this one.

He began his search just like I said earlier, looking for the slave owners with the same last name. He found their wills, estate inventories (which list the names of the enslaved), estate sales papers (which list who bought enslaved people from their deceased's estate), land deeds, slave sales, deeds, census records (for the white Williams family members), and other slave-related records. He built a family tree for this research project, beginning with the first white Williams family member who emigrated from Wales to York County, Virginia.

From there, he traced the various Williams lines into North Carolina, and then into South Carolina, collecting records for each and every white Williams he added to the tree. It was in a series of 1797 Slave Transfer Deeds of Daniel Williams from Pasquotank County, North Carolina, that he found an enslaved man named Moses, as well as a boy slave named Moses. The Deeds enacted an inter-family transfer of Daniel William's enslaved people to various family members in Newberry, South Carolina. He also found several books on the Williams family as well. He started to piece that family together so that he could follow the trail of white Williams children in case the enslaved were passed down to them. I finally jumped in because I couldn't let him do this alone.

The Williams Family of York and Hanover Counties, Virginia.

The Williams family was interesting to me because we didn't start our research with them in the Edgefield area. The first of the Williams family to come to America, or what was then the Virginia colony was John Williams, Sr. Very little is known of this man, apart from settling in York County, Virginia, where all of his children were born. Even the name of his wife remains completely unknown. The family's story really starts with one of his sons, a man known as John "The Wealthy Welshman." John married the Virginia Colony-born Mary Keeling and had eight children. Their names were: John, Mary, Ann, Daniel, Nathaniel, Elizabeth, Sarah, and Joseph. You might ask why was he called the wealthy Welshman? I found a genealogical descendants page and it said the following:

> "Some surmise he earned his wealth like other immigrants to Virginia often did, by growing tobacco. That is possible. He probably was a good wheeler-dealer, made money off that, possibly land as well. But most definitely, the early generations of the family were involved in the distilling of Whiskey. This I am sure is a trade that was brought over from Wales, as it seems to be a popular beverage from all the countries that border the Irish Sea. In fact as late as 1904, the family was advertising the sale of Old Williams Whiskey from their distillery in Williams, Surry County, North Carolina. It states that "The Old Williams Company" of Williams, N.C. was founded in 1768. This business was run by the descendants of John's son Nathaniel (b. 1712). It is probably a family trade handed down over the generations dating much earlier. Just my guess."[53]

All eight of John's children were born in York County, Virginia. Collectively, they would move to Hanover County, Virginia around 1750. Our interest seemed to be moving towards his grandson, Daniel Williams II since this is the person whose name is first associated with Moses. Daniel moved his family from Hanover County, Virginia to Granville County, North Carolina. Daniel and his wife Luanna "Anna" B Henderson-Williams had nine children: Samuel, Davis, Joseph, Frances Elizabeth "Fannie", Nutty, Thomas, Nancy, Polly Washer, and Daniel III.

The Williams research that my cousin Brian gladly took the lead in, shows that we are connected to this family through the Wealthy Welshman's grandson, Daniel Williams II. It was through the deeds, wills, land records and books we learned that property, and sadly human beings, were passed down throughout the family. What was most amazing about this family was the thoroughness of their documentation within the first three generations of arriving in the American colonies. These documents seemed to always have a backup plan for this family.

There was never one owner for anything, and anyone who married into the family would not leave with something or someone they didn't bring to the marriage. This meant women who re-married after the death of their Williams husband forfeited all rights to everything their Williams husbands had bequeathed to them in their respective Wills.

Since slaves were considered property, the early generations of Williams were incredibly thorough with information about their enslaved people. For example, the Williams family listed the ages of those adults who were enslaved. Listing their ages helped us identify which of the enslaved were infants, which were children, those who were childbearing teenagers, those who were adults, and those who were older and elderly. We learned that Moses was given to Maj. John Williams by his nephew Daniel in 1794, and that the age of Moses at that time was twenty-two years old.

Okay, wait twenty-two? My 3x great-grandfather was born around the year this one document was written, so my 3x great grandfather Moses could not have been twenty-two years old. If this was correct, then this was not my 3rd great-grandfather. Originally, I was relieved, but that relief didn't even last a second. We found in the same document another Moses, one of which appeared to be a little boy due to the language used to describe him. Perhaps even a baby. The 1870 census says that my 3x great grandfather Moses was born about 1796.

Finding this information made us realize the 115-year-old Moses wasn't our 3rd great-grandfather, but possibly our 4x great grandfather. We were not expecting this and I went into panic mode. I told Brian *"No, I am not... this cannot... we cannot do this, search!"* Brian was excited and truly ready to move forward. As an African American genealogist, I am as gung-ho to find as many people as possible, just like a genealogist of other races. But truthfully speaking, African Americans know how difficult it is to find our families, whether it is a loss of family because of slavery, names or identity. It is breathtaking and emotionally draining every single time. When you come across mysteries such as this you have to prove it.

It is a need to complete the search to figure out what is right and what is wrong. This find was the reason why Brian reacted just the opposite of me. This story right here was the epitome of what genealogical researching was all about. More importantly, it is stories like these that explain the reason why this book had to be written. Our ancestors were showing once again that they were tired of being forgotten.

So far, I had found two church founders, my 2x great-grandmother – a breeder who went through hell, a 2x great-grand uncle who entered into a form of slavery that was reminiscent to indentured servitude, a young girl who died just because and an entire family that was split up but found each other in the end. Now we were faced with a man who could be the common ancestor of two-thirds of the Edgefield area, as well as large parts of Newberry, Barnwell, and Laurens Counties in South Carolina. Not to mention at least three counties in North Carolina, and possibly two counties in Virginia.

You cannot tell me that their stories should continue to be hidden. If this 115-year-old man was my great grandfather, he lived through the Revolutionary War, the Indian-American Wars, the War of 1812, and the Civil war. He helped his children, his grandchildren and a few of the great-grandchildren live through so much. This was a man who had heard the calls for liberty and freedom from Britain... and lived so long he could enjoy the taste of freedom for himself in 1865. He deserved to be remembered. Who was I to not try to pull his family back together? My heart skipped several beats and, after my meltdown, I was now more determined than ever to find the other forty-four children (we already knew of one because as far as we were concerned, the Moses born in 1796 was the son of the elder Moses Williams.)

Moses and his 45 Children

This project had gone way beyond me and Brian. We decided to pull in some of our other brilliant researching family members and called this The Moses Williams Genetic Genealogy Project. Our cousins Hammad, Lisa, Loretta, Sheila, and Sharon are still combing through a mountain of deeds, documents, newspaper clippings, census records, family history books, probate records, and more. Because of these resources, we knew that Moses Sr. was born in 1769.

We were able to track him being passed down from family member to family member up to 1829. The problem we face in 1829 is a simple one. The last person verified to have enslaved Moses Williams, Sr was Davis Williams. Davis's 1829 probate records are not as specific as the preceding generations of Williams family members. While his Will and estate papers mention the enslaved collectively, no further records have been found which list the enslaved by name, nor what happened to them after he died. We know that this Moses would close the last chapter of his life in Barnwell, South Carolina. The mystery of how he went from Davis Williams' household in Edgefield, to ultimately end up in Barnwell, remains a mystery. We were also able to track Moses Jr.

Most of the Williams' family slaves were kept within the family down the generations. Having this information allows us to establish a pretty accurate timeline as to when Moses Williams, Sr's children were born. If I had to guess, which I did, I would say he had his first child at the age of seventeen, which meant Moses childbearing years went from 1786 to at least 1846. This was a close match in age compared to the newspaper article.

The span of his child producing years presents a picture of my 4x great-grandfather, Moses Williams, Sr, fathering children at the same time that his eldest children were having children – and at the same time as his eldest grandchildren were having children. As well. Put another way, three generations of his family were having children at the same time, this due to the longevity of his life.

This meant that the Jane Williams I wrote about in the previous chapter, who I had listed as my 3x great-grandfather, Moses Williams, Jr., daughter could very well have been his sister. We did find other children, but there would be a lot of DNA work to be done to say whose child they were. This is still an active research project. If I waited for all of the information I needed to write a full history of both Moses Williams, you wouldn't be reading this book now. I began to look at this chapter as a guaranteed follow-up book, or a documentary just about Moses.

Chapter 10 – A Confusing Mix-up

People have often asked me if Ancestry.com works the way its portrayed in its television commercials and online advertising. I can say for me it has, more or less. However, genealogy is the study of individuals. Each individual has his or her story to tell. Discovering that story can be straightforward or exceedingly challenging – and every graduation of difficulty in-between. Sometimes, vital records, documents, and printed stories are easier to find for some ancestors than others. It's a potluck affair. With any service like Ancestry.com, research results will differ for each individual.

What was most beneficial to me was the setup of Ancestry. The basis of this service will always be the family trees that are published through its online platform. The main benefit of this is information sharing. When you begin to create your tree, you start with what you know about your family and build from there. At some point the information that you place on your tree begins to pick up hints or what Ancestry calls "shaky leaves" that will connect you to certain records and possibly even other person's family trees. It is at this point you are able to look at what they have on their tree and compare it to what you have on your tree.

While going over my tree, there was one name I had found that caused me some problems. Her name was Louisa **Adams**. If my information was correct, Louisa was the great aunt to my grandfather, Jefferson Yeldell, on his mother's side of the family. Using what I outlined above, looking at other people's public trees, I was directed to a tree with my Louisa on it. This tree was exactly the same as my tree. Louisa had married a man named Frank **Bugg** and they had fourteen children, but there was a twist. In their tree, my Louisa Adams was listed as Louisa Yeldell.

I sent messages to Ancestry members who had this Louisa in their tree on September 2014, October 2015, and a few additional messages in February and March of 2016. Using my standard research inquiry message, I covered the information that I had found at that point in time. I also stated that I wanted to investigate the name discrepancy between Louisa Yeldell and Louisa Adams. When I first caught this discrepancy, my hypothesis was that the two ladies known as Louisa were one and the same. I just didn't know how.

It wasn't until April of 2016 that a cousin named Joseph spoke with a descendant of Louisa and her husband Frank Bugg. He placed us on a three-way call and she and I spoke briefly. Her name was Karen and she expressed to me that she knew about my Yeldell line and that her hope was to find out more about our connection. She told me the same thing that I found in the Bugg Family trees - that Louisa Yeldell's mother was a woman named Mary Elizabeth Yeldell. She stated that Mary had four children: three girls named Nancy, Harreltine, Louisa and a son named John Yeldell. She went on to say the father was a man named J. H. Yeldell.

This information was so contradictory to what I had found and I expressed that to her. At that point, she shared with me that she was not the overall historian, and invited me to join in on a Bugg family conference call. At that time, I would have the opportunity to speak with the historians and other descendants of Louisa and her husband Frank. She assured me that I was welcome to ask whatever questions I needed to determine who this Louisa was. I told her I would love to join in on the call. The meeting was set for a couple of days later. She sent me the information and I dialed in.

The conference call started with a prayer and introductions of all who were in attendance. From there, they allowed me to talk first. I went straight into who I was and what I knew about my Louisa Adams and the Bugg family. What I shared about Louisa and her family was fairly new because it spoke more about the matriarch of their family. One of their family historians admitted that he did most of his search of the Bugg through the men only. I don't recall him saying why his search was through the men, but I guessed it to be easier to track them than the women of the family. However, learning about the Bugg men had changed the subject off of Louisa for the time being and more on their fabulous matriarch, Louisa's husband Frank's grandmother. They were intrigued as I shared the amazing story of Frank's grandparents: George Quarles and Rebecca Bugg.

George Quarles and Rebecca Bugg

The story of Rebecca **Bugg** and George **Quarles** was a doozy. They were the first family line to provide a physical connection to the white Yeldell's. In Chapter 3, I relayed how my cousin Candace had given me only a possible connection to the white Yeldell family. She was the fourth great-granddaughter of William and Mary Yeldell the family who I thought originally owned my family. George was enslaved by that same Yeldell family that I believe my Yeldell may have come from.

The white Yeldell family was not like any family I had ever researched. Although they had enslaved people, the Yeldell family appeared to ensure their enslaved people had high paying trade jobs like blacksmiths, carpenters, or seamstresses. Then I learned they did something I never thought any enslaver would do: they buried those they enslaved in the same cemetery as they were interred in. Doing that was not a natural occurrence for most slave owners. It was certainly an uncommon practice in Edgefield. I was inclined to say that if you were enslaved in Edgefield during this period of time, the Yeldell family would have been the ones to be owned by.

The daughter of William and Mary was Mary Ann Yeldell. She married a man named Hugh Middleton Quarles. Her dowry included approximately seventeen slaves. One of my oral stories stated that the Yeldells were related to the Quarles. According to this story, a person could see an individual at one point in time with the surname of Quarles, and then see the same person with the surname of Yeldell at another point in time. In other words, one individual swapped between using the last names Yeldell and Quarles. While researching Mary and Hugh, I learned how that may have happened.

Mary and Hugh had a son named William Yeldell Quarles. His name followed a typical family naming pattern for the times. Middle names became common after the American Revolution. The eldest son would normally be named after the father's father, with a middle name connected to a different branch of the family. In this case, the mother's maiden name was used as his middle name. William would sometimes switch between the two surnames. William would go by Yeldell, and then again by Quarles.

His father, Hugh, had an established practice of renting out those he enslaved. According to contemporary documents, several of the big family names that I have found I am related to would increase their income through hiring out their enslaved. The hiring out contracts would provide the enslaved person's occupation, how much was owed to the enslaver, and whom the enslaved person had been rented out. In some cases, this was also a way for those who were enslaved to make money and eventually purchase their own freedom. An enslaved person would hire themselves out for a certain period of time and get paid for their services. This was how I believe Rebecca Bugg met George Quarles.

Rebecca was the first known and documented free person of color (FPOC) that I had come across during the course of my research. There were a few different ways to be considered a FPOC. One was of course through purchasing your own freedom. That was done as I stated above by hiring yourself out and getting a very small portion of the proceeds which an enslaved person would save until they had enough to free themselves. Another way was an enslaved being set free by their enslaver. Although this was not a common thing it did happen. Most enslavers would set free their children or someone they cared for. In the case of Martha, however, her enslaver thought it would be best to continue to provide for her by keeping her enslaved and entrusting her to his wife to take care of her.

My research taught me that even if you did any of those things mentioned above your freedom wasn't guaranteed. You could be stolen and your papers were thrown away. But then I learned the closest way to be guaranteed freedom was to be born free. You had to have been born through a white woman or a mother born from a white woman to be a FPOC. None of the above-mentioned ways to freedom seemed to have applied to anyone in my family.

From the documents that I found, however, Rebecca's mom

was a white woman living in Virginia. There is paperwork that shows her guardian Edward Settles bring a free person of color and children from Virginia to what was then called the 96th District. In 1840, she is still living with her white guardian. This information was definitely interesting, but what was more interesting was learning who her guardian was. Her guardian was the father of my 2x great-grandmother, Mollie Settles. She was married to my 2x great-grandfather Charles Peterson. It was at this point that I was starting to understand it now. Edgefield was so small that there was no way we couldn't be related to everybody.

Records showed that Edward Settles would hire slaves from Hugh Quarles annually. Given the proximity, and property boundaries, between the white Yeldells, Quarles, and Settles, it's not inconceivable that George had been hired out to Edward to provide blacksmith services while he was with the Yeldell family. So, when Mary Yeldell married Hugh Quarles; George was a part of her dowry and the agreement for him providing blacksmith service for Edward continued. This is more than likely how Rebecca and George met and eventually fell in love.

Hugh M. Quarles died and his widow, Mary Ann, was bequeathed the enslaved from her husband's estate. However, an issue that I have yet to find occurred and Mary Ann had to fight for those who were enslaved that she brought into the marriage and the ones she received from her husband. Eventually, she won her case and she was still the owner of George. When Mary Ann remarried, she married a man named Ralsa M. Fuller. It was from Ralsa that Edward Settles purchased George. The Edgefield Slave Records book, written by Gloria Lucas, reported that "George, a mulatto slave man, husband of Rebecca Bugg"[54] was purchased by her Guardian Edward Settles in trust for her daughter Clarissa Bugg. Clarissa was Rebecca's youngest child. Leaving George to her meant that as long as Clarissa outlived Edward, he would not become a slave again. George was now a free man.

He had eleven children with Rebecca while he was enslaved. Their names were: Nancy, Luke, Betsy, Mary, Henry, William, Richard, Hannah, Robert, Clarissa, and Joseph. Mary was the mother of Frank Bugg, who in turn married Louisa. Rebecca died before George, at a date between 1890 and 1900. I haven't found any definitive proof of her death; however, the last document I found stated that George was living as a widow with their son Robert. By this time George was 104 years old.

The conference call was extremely informative for both me and for them. They had not heard the information I shared about Louisa and the Bugg family. The call ended the way it started with one difference we knew our relationship and we knew we were family. As happy as I was about the call I had to figure out what was up with our common relative Louisa Adams or was it, Louisa Yeldell?

Is it Louisa Adams or Louisa Yeldell?

At the conclusion of the Bugg family conference call, the consensus was that Louisa Yeldell and Louisa Adams were one in the same person. My new task was to develop a research methodology in order to prove it. I first had to look at the known facts:

- **Fact #1** – The given parents for the two Louisa's were different. The parents of Louisa Adams were cited as Henry Adams and Nancy (maiden name unknown) in the 1870 federal census, while only one parent was cited in Louisa Yeldell. This was her mother, Elizabeth;
- **Fact #2** – If the Elizabeth who was Louisa Yeldell's mother, and the Nancy who was Louisa Adam's mother were one in the same woman, the dates of birth were markedly different between the two; and
- **Fact #3** – I couldn't compare my Henry to the J.H. Yeldell that the Bugg family spoke of because I hadn't seen where he connected yet. These types of differences, although seemingly not that big, can make a huge difference in determining the truth.

After thinking about how Louisa Adams and Louisa Yeldell might be the same person, I experienced an epiphany. It was a moment similar to the one when I realized that my 2nd great-grandmother Jane Senior, from Chapter 8 was listed twice on the 1870 Federal Census. I reviewed the 1870 census that my Louisa Adams was on and sure enough, on August 17th, Louisa Yeldell was listed with her mother Elizabeth and her siblings. And, on August 18th, Louisa Adams was listed with Ezra's parents, Henry and Nancy Adams. Henry or Nancy had to be Elizabeth's siblings.

    I started to look at the children of both sets of parents. In doing so, I noticed that Elizabeth had a daughter named Nancy, while Henry and Nancy had a daughter named Elizabeth. I checked out how people in colonial times named their children and found this:

- the first daughter is named after the mother's mother
- the second daughter is named after the father's mother
- the third daughter is named after the mother herself
- and the fourth through end daughter is named after a favorite sister or friend (usually of the mothers)[55]

Although I had not found definitive proof, it was my educated guess that Nancy Adams and Elizabeth Yeldell were siblings.

It was also likely that Louisa was not an Adams, but a Yeldell. This meant that the people I had originally thought were her siblings were actually her first cousins. This included my 2nd great-grandfather, Ezra Adams. It was learning information like this that made the subtitle to this book. Once again, I was being thrown back into a family name that I had already had a connection too. My family connected twice, maybe even three times over to the Petersons, Yeldells, Settles, Holloways, Seniors and more.

Chapter 11 – John Yeldell a.k.a Rev. Elijah F. Flemon

There was a bit more information that was shared with me during the conference call. They told me that Louisa Yeldell's brother, John Yeldell was a man who was involved in a well-known trial back in 1884. The trial was about a black man who disappeared for five years after the crime of killing a white man. When found in Pennsylvania, he was brought back to South Carolina to stand trial. The reason why John Yeldell was able to disappear for so long was a simple one: he changed his identity. At the time he was found, John was a preacher who went by the name of Elijah F. Flemon.

The Rev. E.F. Flemon, a.k.a John Yeldell was my mother's 2nd great-grandmother Nancy Adams nephew. As I researched his life story, I realized that John Yeldell should have been taught in American history books. His story was significant in showing what lengths the South would go to in wielding power over people of color in the period between the Reconstruction in 1877 and the progressively harsher constraints of the Jim Crow Era at the turn of the 20th Century. An accusation of murder levied against a black man in the South was tantamount to a death sentence; especially if the victim was white. This was especially true if you were a black man in South Carolina. People of color had been lynched for far lesser reasons, including merely being successful business people, Take the lynching of Anthony Crawford for example.

Anthony Crawford was said to have been the richest African American in the Abbeville area (once part of the 96th District) due to owning over 400 acres of land. He was known for having a zero-tolerance for disrespectful people and was heard by many saying, "the day a white man hits me will be the day I die." That statement proved true for him on the 21 October 1916 due to a disagreement for the cost of products he wanted to pay Anthony was hit over the head and for his safety placed in jail. However, the people didn't want him to get away, so they overtook the jail kidnapped, beat, dragged and hung Anthony's body using it for target practice.

Like Anthony's, John's predicament must have been extremely scary. The incident in question happened in 1884, around an especially contentious, rancorous, and toxic presidential election between Republican candidate, James G. Blaine, and the Democratic candidate, Grover Cleveland. In conducting this research, the first thing I had to do was prove whether John and the good Reverend appeared in the same set of records at the same time during the same time period. Or, whether I could find one man for one block of time, who then disappeared, followed by the sudden appearance of another man in a subsequent block of time.

I took my usual route when searching for John Yeldell. I began my search with the U.S. Census records and found him in 1870, where he was living with his mother and sisters. One of those sisters was Louisa Yeldell-Bugg from the previous chapter. I found him again in 1880 as a servant to a John T. Johnston. The 1880 census was the end of the line for John Yeldell. I could find nothing further for him. He had disappeared into the ether. As a matter of fact, his mom and two sisters had disappeared as well. The only person from his family that could still be found was his sister Louisa, who, by the 1880s, now had the married name, Louisa Bugg.

I began developing a theory and this was a good sign. If he had changed his name due to the incident, then it would be only natural for an Elijah F. Flemon to begin to appear sometime in the 1900s. This made me begin my search for Reverend Flemon and to see if he existed the same time as John Yeldell. I checked for an Elijah Flemon in every state but my primary searches were done in South Carolina and Pennsylvania. I couldn't find him anywhere before 1910 in Pennsylvania; he simply did not exist prior to that. Although both men didn't appear to exist at the same time, it still wasn't proof enough.

I contacted the Edgefield archives to request John Yeldell's trial papers. However, no one ever got back to me. I began searching for articles about the case through a website called Newspapers.com. This site is the online home of 200+ million pages of historical newspapers from 4,900+ newspapers from around the United States and beyond. Newspapers provide a unique view of the past and can help us understand and connect with the people, events, and attitudes of an earlier time.[56] Before I go any further, let me explain how the search works for this site.

Let's say you type in the name John Yeldell. The website will display results for every newspaper with the name John, Yeldell, or any variation of the name. I am explaining this because, with over 200+ million pages, you must be as accurate as possible with your search. With that being said, I typed the search string "John Yeldell" and "1884" in the search box. The site returned 26 matches. The first article that popped up was "A full and true account of the Edgefield trouble, A correct statement of the Killing of the Constable Blackwell by a gang of Negro desperados – No further trouble Anticipated." When I read the article that followed, I knew this was a story that I had to find out about. The story reads as follows:

"A FULL AND TRUE ACCOUNT OF THE EDGEFIELD TROUBLE

A correct statement of the Killing of the Constable Blackwell by a gang of Negro desperados – No further trouble Anticipated

(Charleston Sunday News)

Augusta, GA., November 1 – Mr. B.W. Bettis Jr., of Edgefield, the chairman of the Democratic executive committee of that county passed through Augusta today on his way home from Parksville. He states that all is now quiet at that place and there is no danger of further trouble. The feeling however, throughout Edgefield is very feverish, but he considers that this feeling is the best guarantee of safety and peace. His object in going to Parksville was to ascertain the truth about the trouble. The difficulty began last Saturday when six rough looking negroes entered Mr. Parks store in the village and began abusing a democratic negro who was present. They then went out and walked some distance and fired off their pistols. Sunday morning

Mr. Parks met one of the negroes name[sic] Yeldell on the street and asked him what he meant by his conduct in the store the night before. Yeldell said he meant nothing. Parks then told him that if he ever came to his store and acted that way again he would break a stick over his head. He then charged him with having a pistol. Yeldell at first denied this, but Press Blackwell came up and started to search him when the negro jerked out his pistol and flourished it in the air. The other five who were with him the night before also came up and exhibited pistols. On Wednesday, Mr. Parks, who is a trial justice, issued a warrant for the arrest of the six negroes on the charge of carrying concealed weapons and put it in the hands of James Blackwell to serve. Accompanied by three others Blackwell went out to where the negroes, lived but they had been informed of his coming and waited in the bushes. When the posse came up the negroes fired a volley, all apparently aiming at Blackwell, as nobody else was struck. The posse returned the fire. Several other negroes, armed with guns, now rushed up, but were arrested by the posse. The ones who did the shooting escaped and have not yet been found. Those that were arrested were sent to Edgefield jail. Blackwell died Thursday, and was buried yesterday. The vicinity of Parksville has been picketed by white men every night, and last night a white man named Hitt, who approached one of the pickets in the dark, was fired upon by the latter and slightly wounded in the arm, the picket supposing that one of the negroes was creeping up to him. The following named negroes are the six ringleaders still at lalge[sic], and for whom active search is being made: Joseph Briggs five feet eight inches high, 28 years of age: John Yeldell 5 feet 6 inches high, 28 years old, scar on the right cheek: Allen Harris 5 feet 8 inches high, 22 years of age: Elijah Briggs 5 feet 10 inches high, 21 years of age: Sam Harris 5 feet 7 inches high, 24 years of age; Has Kilcrease 5 feet 6 inches high, 21 years of age."[57]

It sounds interesting, right? Well, there is much more and it is jaw-dropping. This story was so incredible there will be some instances where I will not be able to paraphrase. I will have to share the story straight from the source. The language of these accounts is so coded, so nuanced, that the original text has been included. If you see misspelled words or grammatical errors, within these original accounts, please bear in mind these are the actual press accounts that were documented during that time.

My first impression of the story above left me with a lot of questions. For instance, John's response to the incident seemed nonchalant, almost as if he didn't have a clue of what Mr. Parks was talking about. Was he even in the store when the said incident occurred? And why did Mr. Parks jump from threatening him with "beating him over the head with a stick" to charging him with having a gun? There were other areas of the story where inconsistencies jumped out at me, however, these were the ones that stood out the most. I had to find more stories because I was beginning to realize just how huge this story was.

The magnitude of the story wasn't surprising in and of itself. Here we are in the early decades of the Jim Crow Era and the Klu Klux Klan, and a black man has the audacity to kill a white man in an area still very upset that they lost the war. My cousin Natonne spoke about this story as the Parksville riot. Her interest in this story was about the morale of Edgefield's black population, and how our families lived through that time. She had given me information about Judge Parks, and how the white citizens of that town vowed that they would do what it took to keep it white. I do not remember if she said the story was about a Yeldell. I knew more articles were out there, and I needed to find them. Just as I thought, there were more, a staggering amount more. I went back to my original search parameters again and pulled up the 26 search results in order to read the other articles. In doing so, I found the story below. This time, the story began to change.

"The Parksville Tragedy

The following account of a murderous affair at Parksville, Edgefield County, is copied from the Edgefield Advertiser:

On Saturday night the 25th of October it seems that six negroes commenced to abuse a colored man in a store next door to Mr. Robert Park's because the offending negro professed to be a Democrat. They used insulting language and finally just walked off, from the store firing their pistols. Sunday morning Mr. Parks saw one of the parties, Jno. Yeldell by name, and upbraided him about his conduct of the night before. The other negroes joined Yeldell, and being asked by Mr. Parks if they were not armed, responded they were and all displayed their pistols. Mr. Parks then issued a warrant against these parties for carrying concealed weapons, and Mr. James Blackwell was deputed as constable to serve them. With two or three aids he surrounded a house where the negroes were supposed to be to affect their arrest. They hid however, in ambush and fired upon Blackwell, riddling him with buckshots and inflicting wounds from which he has since died. About thirty rounds, it is said were fired, but no one else was hurt. Seven other negroes came up, attracted by the firing, and were arrested by the whites. These seven with two others, have been brought to our town and lodged in our jail, where they still are. They have not demanded a hearing.

Those who fired the fatal volley however, ran off, and these are the parties who are now being anxiously looked for.

In an editorial the Advertiser says:

The ringleader's in the savage and wanton Parksville tragedy have not yet been caught, but a party of earnest and determined white men are continuing the search for them. It is thought they have crossed the Savannah river, which is near Parksville.

And when these barbarous and bloody black bullies shall be apprehended, there is a way of dealing with them which need involve no outraged citizen in any way. Let the strong, silent, steady footsteps of the law overtake these men and show them and their companions what it is to set themselves up against the law of the land. Such Impudent tongues, stupid heads and bloody hands seldom escape punishment. There is but one proper end to such an act. The men who perpetrated it must be hanged until they are dead, dead, dead!"[58]

Now, this was interesting. The incident had gone from being within Mr. Parks' store to occurring on the property next door to Parks. There was also no mention of the threat of John being bashed in the head. As a matter of fact, the story jumped straight to John and his comrades having guns, and completely different from the supposed "true accounts". The exaggerations around the incident, to make a bad situation worse, had begun. While searching through the 26 articles, I came across another case involving yet another Yeldell that happened around the same time. What made it interesting was that this Yeldell was white. See the story below:

Serious and Sad

Selma times.

While on his usual rounds yesterday, The Times reporter learned of a serious difficulty, which occurred near Snow Hill on Wednesday last, and in which Col. J.W. Stein, an old and highly respected citizen of Wilcox County, was wounded, perhaps fatally, by young Mr. Willie R Yeldell.

From the information gathered it seems that the gentlemen had been to Snow Hill and while there became involved in a dispute. They left Snow Hill, however, together, and it was presumed that all differences had been amicably settled. When several miles from town on their way home, the dispute was revived, and ended in a difficulty. Mr. Yeldell fired upon Mr. Stein with a shotgun loaded with a bird shot, inflicting painful wounds and filling the unfortunate man's face with shot. It was reported yesterday that Col. Stein was in a critical condition and that both eyes were out from the wounds. Mr. Yeldell, the young man who did the shooting, is a nephew of Col. Stein, the man whom he wounded.

The sad occurrence is universally regretted, as Col. Stein was a gallant soldier in the late war, an honored man and highly respected citizen. Mr. Yeldell is also respected as an upright gentlemanly young man. Whisky, the champion curse of this age, is supposed to have been the prime cause of the sad affair.[59]

Well, that was different. I reproduced this article to show you the mindset of the south during this post-Reconstruction Era period. President Johnson came up with a solution in order for the south to abide by the Constitution specifically, the 13th Amendment which abolished slavery, and still allow state governments to make certain rules that applied to the individual states. His plan to keep the states from trying to secede from the Union was for all states to keep their loyalty to the Union and pay off war debts; in return, the states, specifically the southern states, could rebuild in their own way or have state laws. That way was called the black codes. These were laws designed to restrict freed blacks' activity and ensure their availability as a labor force now that slavery had been abolished.[60] It was because of these codes that John was affected and the White Yeldell in Alabama was not.

Yeldell Arrested

I wanted to find further articles by narrowing my search to South Carolina. Adjusting the search to cover this specific parameter, Newspaper.com reduced the number of articles to thirteen. I did something different and decided to change my search parameter completely. I dropped South Carolina, while keeping the name John Yeldell, then changed the date range from 1884 only for the period between1884 and 1890. I hit pay dirt. There were over 500 articles pertaining to this case. There were articles covering the length and breadth of the continental United States: from South Carolina to Idaho.

As I read each published account, I felt like I was sitting in a movie theater watching this entire story unfold. I read every single one and saved over 120 articles total. These articles allowed me to see things from both sides. I am not saying from a black and white perspective but from a North and South perspective. Reading these articles explained why my Edgefield families had departed South Carolina for points north, east, and west – everywhere barring the South - during the Great Migration.

Most of the returns from my Newspaper.com search were papers from 1889. I sorted the articles from the oldest first. It was the articles from 1889 that gave me a complete story. John had disappeared after the riot for what seems to have been five years. The papers talked about everything from his arrest to the US Government's involvement, to the trial and, finally, the verdict. By the time I read the 1889-published "true account", the one article that featured Jon's own words, this story was virtually unrecognizable. John's account bore little resemblance to the bulk of news stories that had been published across the country. Below is the first article I found after John was found and arrested in 1889.

"ACCUSED OF MURDER

A Colored Minister Arrested on a Serious Charge

Pittsburgh, July 9. – Rev. E. F. Flemon, alias John Yeldell who has been acting as pastor of the Arthur Street Wesley Church (colored) or some time, has been arrested on a charge of murder. Sheriff Lyon of Edgefield, S.C., telegraphs to the police here that Flemon or Yeldell, had been implicated in a brutal murder in that county in 1886 but had fled at the time and had not been heard of until a short time ago, when through a letter addressed to somebody in that locality, it was learned that he had located in this vicinity. The prisoner is an unusually bright and well educated colored man and betrays no signs of nervousness over his arrest He has been regarded as a very exemplary man and minister by the colored people."[61]

This was a clipping from a northern paper called ***The Buffalo Commercial***, published in Buffalo, NY. The story seemed to have quite a number of assumptions, however, it still came across as fair. The journalist didn't claim that the killer was John, and the paper left some room for the idea that this could be a case of mistaken identity. The journalist's argument was that the case hadn't been made that John Yeldell and Rev. Elijah Flemon was the same man. As a matter of fact, the only thing that was different was the year the incident occurred. But given the fact that it is five years later, information could be provided incorrectly. When I read about the arrest in a southern paper you, could not only see but feel, the difference in the reporting. ***The Abbeville Press and Banner*** reported the following:

Something About Yeldell

McCormick News

A few days ago the Augusta Chronicle contained a telegraphic account of the arrest of John Yeldell, in Pittsburgh, Pennsylvania, charged with murder in Edgefield County in 1886.

The occasion is well remembered in this section as the Parksville riot. There was disorder in this Edgefield town and a negro was arrested. The negroes defled the law and liberated the prisoner. A posse of white men tried to re-arrest the negro and were met with a volley from a body of negroes, in which young Blackwell was killed.

Several negroes were arrested and four were tried at Edgefield and convicted of murder. They subsequently got a new trial, however, and were acquitted, but they left the country. John Yeldell, who was believed to be the leader in the insurrection, made his escape and was never arrested. He had never been heard of since the riot.

The other day a disturbance occurred in a negro family in Parksville and, after a row between father and son, the old man's barn was burned, Suspicion pointed to the son, and he was arrested. When searched a letter was found in his pocket from John Yeldell, at Pittsburgh.

It takes a long time on some occasions, but murder will out".[62]

Could you feel the difference as you read the story? They knew it was him simply because of the telegraph that was sent, and the letter that was found. There was no waiting for a visual confirmation. Also, did you see how the story changed completely? There was no store, there was no one being picked on because he was a Negro Democrat, and no guns being fired in the air. As a matter of fact, the date of when the incident occurred was different in this article as well. If it was 'well remembered', why was the date given as 1886? And who was arrested that the "Negroes" needed to save? If they hadn't said it was the Parksville Riot, I would have thought this was another incident. I had to make myself focus on the research, but I will admit I started to wonder if John wasn't the "Negro" that had been harassed. I knew there was more to this than I knew.

The arresting officer, Inspector McAleese in Pittsburgh, wanted to be fair. Although the physical description of the murder suspect seemed to match Elijah Flemon, he couldn't hold the man based on just that piece of information. A telegraph was sent to Sheriff Lyons from Inspector McAleese in Pittsburgh to let him know that he had until the Saturday to come and identify the prisoner, and that he needed to bring the

Figure 19 - Deputy Lyon, Photo courtesy of The Pittsburgh Press c. 1889

necessary papers as well to retrieve him. Because of the distance during that era, it was harder to get there. The governors of both South Carolina and Pennsylvania were added into the mix. Governor Beaver of Pennsylvania stepped in:

"FLEMON MUST BE HELD

Governor Beaver Request the Authorities to Detain Him

Last night the police authorities of this city received a dispatch from Governor Beaver dated Harrisburg, instructing them to hold John Yeldell until papers arrived for him.

The man referred to is Rev. E.F. Flemon, who, it is alleged, is wanted at Edgefield SC for murder. After the hearing before Judge Ewing on Tuesday he was remanded to jail. Inspector McAleese telegraphed to Thomas J. Lyon, who first sent word here, telling him of the disposition of the case. The Inspector notified Lyon to be in this city on Saturday when the argument takes place, with papers, etc., to prove his charge. The distance is so great that Lyon could not arrive in time. So he sent a telegram to the Inspector telling him to hold Yeldell at all hazards. Mr. Lyon, fearing that the prisoner might escape, consulted the Governor of South Carolina, and it was on the request of that official that Governor Beaver sent the telegram instructing the authorities to hold the prisoner. This telegram will be produced in court to-morrow, and the Inspector thinks it is sufficient to cause the detention of the prisoner."[63]

The Fight to Extradite Yeldell

Put simply, John was literally arrested after preaching from the pulpit, and placed in Jail until the officers from Edgefield could come and identify him. When the deputies arrived, they were not able to identify him right away, possibly due to the lateness of the hour when they arrived. They did, however, go to see the man known as Elijah Flemon, to the people of Pittsburgh, the next day.

When Edgefield County, Marshall Strom went to identify John, the best scene of the movie (did I say movie?) was being played out at this point.

Excerpt from "PARSON FLEMON'S STORY
THE MOST TALKED-OF COLORED MAN IN THE LAND.

HIS ARREST IN CHURCH AND THE COMPLICATIONS ATTENDING HIS EXTRADITION TO SOUTH CAROLINA.

There were ten colored prisoners in the Allegheny County jail the day the Deputies called. They were of all shades, sizes and ages. Through the influence of Friends Yeldell was allowed to don another man's apparel, and when the ten prisoners were drawn up in line he appeared in the ragged clothes and slouch hat of a vagrant his own neat black suit and glossy hat being upon a footpad. The identification was, however, unmistakable complete. Marshall Strom without looking at the others, walked right up to the fugitive, and extending his hand, exclaimed: "John Yeldell! John Yeldell! Howdy!" The prisoner dropped his head and refused to speak. "All right sah," said the Palmetto officer, "but I know you John, and I'll shake hands just the same," and he did so with vigor".[64]

Figure 20 - Deputy Strom, Photo courtesy of The Pittsburgh Press c. 1889

Tell me you didn't see that as you read it play out in your head. This story had everything drama, suspense, and action. When that happened, the officers thought they could just walk away into the sunset with John, but there was a problem. The arraignment judge, Judge Ewing, appears to have been a fair judge. He stated that Flemon should not have been held based on a telegram only.

He was ready to let him go. A habeas corpus or a motion was filed to ensure that John would be brought to court to determine if he was being held illegally. This move would soon bring the government into the action:

"OUT FOR AN AIRING,

And Then Sent Back to Jail for Final Disposition Next Wednesday – That is Rev. Mr. Flemon's Fix.

The habeas corpus case of Rev. E. F. Flemon, alias Yeldell, was brought to Judge Ewings attention yesterday. Clarence Burleigh, Esq., counsel, presented a telegram to the Chief of Police, signed James A. Beaver, stating that requisition papers were on the way and Yeldell should be held until they arrived.

Judge Ewing seemed to regard the telegram as a fake, as he said Governor Beaver was a lawyer and should know that unless proper evidence was presented as to the identity of Flemon, alias Yeldell, he could not be held on a telegram.

Mr. Burleigh then asked that the case be continued until next Wednesday, stating that if sufficient evidence to hold could not be had at that time no further objection to release would be urged, and the prisoner's counsel had agreed to a continuance, if the Rev. Flemon be permitted to preach in the county jail to-day.

Mr. McKenna said while he might not strenuously object to a continuance, yet his man stood on his legal right. If the Judge felt the telegram was sufficient on which to hold Flemon they submitted, but with the suggestion that Flemon denied that he was Yeldell, and there was no evidence to show Governor Beaver sent the message, which fact should have gravity.

Judge Ewing finally decided to hold the accused

until Wednesday morning 9 o'clock, stating that if at that time the South Carolina people could not show that he was Yeldell he would be discharged, and the prisoner was locked up again. The Central station officers say that they can learn nothing of the case as the prisoner doesn't yield under any kind of pressure."[65]

As the article above stated, Flemon never gave any information. Even when he was identified, he refused to speak. There was now the matter of the extradition to deal with. John's church, the John Wesley Church of Arthur Street, temporarily denied any acquaintance with him. They went as far as to place an article in the paper disassociating itself with him. They did this, however, before they knew how unfairly John was being treated. Once they found out, it was like a war was being waged. A meeting was called and the following article shows the actions they took after they realized the unfair treatment that John was receiving.

WILL STAND BY FLEMON.

SYMPATHY FOR THE IMPRISONED COLORED PREACHER.

A Meeting in Franklin School Last Night at Which Some Strong Speeches Were Made – Money Raised and Resolutions Passed.

Seventy-five colored persons, representing all the churches of the hill, met in Franklin school house, Seventh ward, last night and passed resolutions demanding justice for Rev. E. F. Flemon. The latter is charged with murder committed in South Carolina, and two officers from that state are here ready to take him back.

The Rev. George W. Clinton, pastor of the John Wesley Church, of Arthur Street, called the meeting to order. After he had announced the object of it, permanent officers were chosen. Mr. Clinton declined to be chairman and R. W. Jenkins was elected. James C. Delphy was elected secretary and B.T. Stewart was appointed reporter for the meeting. Mr. Clinton corrected the statement that Flemon had been the pastor of a church here, and was arrested just as he finished preaching. Mr. Clinton himself is pastor of the church of which it was said Flemon was the minister. He cautioned those present not to be rash, and said that they only wanted Flemon to get a fair and impartial trial. No stone was to be left unturned to prove his innocence. If he was guilty he should be punished, but if he was innocent he should be released. No two men could come to Pittsburgh and take away a black man to a state like South Carolina until he was proven guilty, especially when the men who came from that State bragged that they had only lynched six negroes since the emancipation.

Resolutions were then presented by Mr. Clinton. They recited the facts that Flemon has been living in the city for the past three years, and that he was wanted for murder in Edgefield county, South Carolina. As he bears papers showing him to have been a preacher there, as he has had a good character here; as his friends believe he can prove his innocence. They furthermore resolved to use every effort in their power to keep him in the city until conclusive evidence of his guilt is furnished. And thanked the judges for their attitudes in the habeas corpus proceedings.

The resolutions were discussed and spirited language was used. Of a dozen speakers all denounced the course that had been pursued as unjust. All were bitter against South Carolina, stating that the black man could not receive justice there, and that if Flemon was taken there he would be hung, guilt or innocent. Those who spoke were Messrs. Richard Keys, John H. Chilton, Watson, Foster, Holland, D.M. Watson, Robert Ray, Rev.

J.H. McMullen, Rev. D. S. Bentley, and Scott Taper.

J. H. Chilton grew eloquent and said he would defend Flemon if he lost his life of position, and any colored man who would not stand up for the colored race was a coward. He varied the proceedings somewhat by asking the meeting to endorse a letter to Chief J. O. Brown complaining of the conduct of Detective Sol Coulson. It was stated that Coulson, while at the jail, yesterday, when Flemon was being identified, called Chilton harsh names.

Mr. Watson spoke vehemently. He said that if Flemon shot the man in cold blood, let him hang, but if he killed him in self-defense, let them all die for him.

Mr. Chilton offered to be one of a party to prevent Flemon going back at any rate. His suggestion, however, did not meet with favor, an amicable course being the popular one.

A sum of money was raised and a committee appointed to retain counsel for Flemon.[66]

Reading this made me feel a little better. I was relieved John was not facing this alone after all. He wasn't talking. Only the law enforcement officers knew anything about him, or at least they thought they did, and what they did know was possibly a lie. As a matter of fact, it was beginning to come out that they were lying. There were several problems that surfaced during the identification process which delayed the extradition process. The date of the incident was false and, John's lawyer pointed out that if the incident happened in 1886, that there was proof that John was living in the north at that time. There was also an issue with the extradition papers. Judge Ewing believed the extradition papers hadn't really come from Governor Beaver. If they did, there was no date cited within the extradition order, no victims' names were given, and no indictment order had been included. This was a huge omission. What I found to be really funny was the new way the story that was now being shared about the day the murder happened. The following is the story of what happened, according to Edgefield County Marshal Strom:

"Except from FLEMON IS BADLY WANTED.
REQUISITION PAPERS FOR THE COLORED PREACHER.

He is said to be a Murderer and a Very Bad Man by the authorities of South Carolina – Nature of the Crime.

The story of the murder for which Yeldell, alias Flemon, is wanted was told yesterday by Deputy Sheriff Strom. Yeldell was raised from a boy by ex-Governor Sheppard, of South Carolina, and was always considered a leader of a tough gang, as was his father before him. Said the deputy sheriff: "Yeldell worked for me on my plantation for several years and he always gave me trouble. He was the ringleader of a crowd of nine colored men who, on Sunday morning, October 27, 1884, got drunk and created a disturbance in Parkesville, Edgefield county. They fired revolvers on the streets, frightened white ladies and terrorized the people generally. The next day warrants were sworn out against them for rioting, and Deputy Sheriff Blackwell was authorized to serve them, but the men heard of it, and left for the swamps nearby, where they remained until Tuesday night. Blackwell heard of their return, and taking a couple of men with him started for an old cabin in which the men were hiding, about a mile from town. When they got within a few yards of the building the inmates open fire on them with shot guns. Blackwell, fell dead on the spot, his body fairly riddled with buckshots. The other men fled, and the next morning the negroes had all escaped to the swamps again. Subsequently two of them were captured, tried and convicted of murder, which means hanging in that State, but they managed to secure a new trial and succeeded in placing the responsibility for the killing on John Yeldell, who was known to have had two double barreled shotguns and a revolver before the murder occurred, and both were acquitted."[67]

Okay! So, what was this? This was not the "true accounts". This was the story that was said during the identification of Flemon as being Yeldell. This is the account which caused Judge Ewing to pause, and investigate further. If you notice, in the story, he gave the real date of the incident. It was this story, and others that followed, which caused the ruckus. From the date to the number of men involved, it was all different, and everything had to be reviewed. One of the rare times that John did speak, he expressed what would happen if he left with the two Deputy Sheriffs to return to South Carolina to face trial:

"Yeldell does not want to go South. He says for the Blackwell crime two men have been reported hanged, two lynch[sic], and two acquitted, and he knows of two more who were thrown in the river – John Talbot and Frederick Harris – both of whom were Republicans. "I would be willing to go back all right," he says, "but not with those deputies. Those fellows will not take me back to South Carolina. They will leave me dead between this and the station. I would go with a Union man, if he were no bigger than a mouse and tied me with a thread, but with these men, whose records I know, no."[68]

The U.S. Government Gets Involved

Due to the poor handling of the case on the prosecution side, things were looking better for John, and bad for South Carolina. The African Americans in the Pittsburg area felt like John; if he traveled to South Carolina, would be killed as soon as his feet touched South Carolina soil. The goal at this point was to get as much publicity for him as possible and make him a political refugee of the State of South Carolina and hopefully can get a new trial venue. The people of Pittsburgh and John's lawyers pulled out all the stops. They petitioned to go to the highest court in

Pennsylvania; the Supreme Court. They also requested federal aid from the county representative, Congressman John Dalzell. Going to Dalzell was a good idea because they got his attention in a way that I don't think they were expecting.

Excerpts from "FLEMON IS YELDELL

The Political Refugee is Charged With Murdering a Negro Chaser.

THE PRESIDENT IS ASKED

By Congressman Dalzell to Bring Federal Machinery to Bear.

THE STARTLING STORY OF THE MURDER IN THE CONGRESSMAN'S OFFICE

The office of Mr. Dalzell was reached at 1:30 o'clock yesterday afternoon, and after a few preliminaries the genial representative from Pittsburgh asked why the committee came to him.

"We want you to save the life of a Southern Republican, now a political refugee from his native State," solemnly answered Rev. G. W. Clinton.

"But," said Mr. Dalzell, somewhat astonished, "from all I can hear, this murder is alleged to have been committed in 1886, an 'off' year, politically."

"That statement is designedly wrong," said the spokesman of the committee. "The omission of the date in Governor Richardson's requisition was a portion of the plan to take this man's life for a political murder. The fact is that the killing of James Blackwell was an incident of the Blaine-Cleveland campaign, and happened on Monday, October 28, 1884, just a week and a day before election. Here is Rev. McMullen, Mr. Congressman, who was living in Chester county, S. C., during that year, and was in Edgefield county during that time of the killing, and can tell you the whole story of the Death of

Blackwell."[69]

The congressman listened to Rev. McMullen's story which was yet a different variation of the ones we heard before.

"Excerpts from FLEMON IS YELDELL
A RACE WAR GRAPHICALLY SKETCHED.

Political excitement was at fever heat in Edgefield county, for the negroes thereabout idolized Mr. Blaine. There had be frequent bloodless conflicts between the races during the month of October, and the trouble culminated on Sunday morning a week and two days before election day.

As a party of colored men, among whom was Mr. Flemon, were going home from church, a party of whites, heavily armed, met them, and passed the colored men cursing them roundly. At the distance of a few hundred feet the white men fired playfully at the colored men, and a minie ball passed through Flemon's hat. The colored men were frightened and scattered, and the white men ran amuck, claiming that the colored men were armed.

On the next day a dozen or more colored men were working in the fields, with Flemon again among them. A gang of white men rode into the field and chased the colored men into the woods, firing at them repeatedly. The fugitives pushed on for several miles, and, when night fell, took refuge in the gin house on a white man's farm. Some slept, while others kept watch anxiously. At nearly daybreak, the baying of bloodhound betokened the approach of the white party, and it was deemed useless to attempt an escape.

FLEMON LED IN PRAYER

It was determed to defend themselves, and, after looking to their guns, the colored men held a prayer meeting, over which Flemon presided. Dawn was just breaking, when the whites opened fire, and the colored men responded. A lively fusilade followed, in the course Flemon was shot through the arm, causing a compound fracture of the bone.

The whites hurriedly decamped after a raking volley fired by the colored men, and it was afterward learned that James Blackwell, a white lad aged 18, and not at that time or any other a deputy sheriff, had been mortally wounded and died the same day while being hurried back to his home. He was, therefore, not an officer of the law, and did not die in the discharge of his official duty as has been claimed. Several colored men of the party were killed and wounded. But I wish to emphasize the fact that there was not a legally authorized deputy sheriff in the white party."[70]

Now before I go any further, can I point out that the conversation and language being held above? This does not sound like someone of no intelligence; a person who had just come out of slavery 25 years previously. Some of these men were born into slavery during the 1850s, a time when schooling was not afforded to people of color, and yet they seemed to be well educated. Nevertheless, they went on to explain that Governor Richardson "has chosen to add insult to injury" because he deputized Marshal Bert Strom, and he was a part of the group of white men that night. Congressman Dalzell listened and he had a response that same day.

"Excerpts from FLEMON IS YELDELL.

CONGRESSMAN DALZELL'S REPLY.

The very remarkable turn affairs have taken interest me extraordinarily, both as an individual and as a United States Representative. If counsel will embody a statement of the facts detailed by Rev. McMullen, showing the political complexion of the crime and the circumstances, I will personally and at once lay the same before the Attorney General and the Senators from

Pennsylvania, and request that powers of the Federal Government, so far as legal, be invoked to see that, if the prisoner is returned to South Carolina, he be given as fair a trial as if he were a white man."[71]

WOW! This court case had just become nationally known. The Attorney General and the Senators of Pennsylvania were now being brought into the mix. Mr. McKenna, who was one of Yeldell's lawyers, quickly wrote up what the congressman asked for and got it into his hands. The congressman then informed them that he would involve his lawyer friend who was now head of the Department of Justice. Dalzell would also inform President Harrison, the President of the United States at the time.

This is why this story should have been in our history books. It was as famous as the Dred Scott case (March 1857) and as well-known as Nat Turner's rebellion (August 1831). While Dalzell was trying to get the United States Government involved, Yeldell's lawyers were seeking the help of the Supreme Court in Pennsylvania. Neither persons were trying to stop the trial itself, but the venue in which it would be held, which was South Carolina. Because the case had become so large, so did the cost. **The Pittsburgh Times** wrote,

> "The Pittsburgh Times will guarantee, in accordance with the foregoing, the expenses of carrying the E.F. Flemon case to and through the Supreme Court of Pennsylvania. Those who desire to share in giving a black man a white man's chance for his life are welcome, though not absolutely necessary."[72]

With the inclusion of Pennsylvania Senators, the Attorney General, and the POTUS, Yeldell had become as well-known as Frederick Douglas himself. **The Abbeville Press and Banner** said the same thing:

> "John Yeldell, of Edgefield and Pittsburgh, who for several weeks has been "a bigger man" than that other distinguished represented of the negro race in

America, Fred Douglas."[73]

If the lawyers, and the Friends of Yeldell, could pull this off, this would stop the extradition. If successful, a new trial venue would have made South Carolina look bad. It would also make both the Governor of Pennsylvania and the Governor of South Carolina people who were not men of their word. The Government didn't intercede. The Pennsylvania Supreme Court did not grant the writ. Together, both failures meant Yeldell was going to South Carolina. In one hand the South Carolinians were overjoyed.

"YELDELL WILL COME BACK

The Pennsylvania Supreme Court Refuses to Grant the Writ Sued For.

Philadelphia, July 25 – The Supreme Court refuses to grant the writ sued for in the case of Rev. Mr. Flemon, the colored pastor of Pittsburgh, who is wanted in South Carolina for murder.

Flemon's counsel and citizens of Pittsburgh to-day appealed to Governor Beaver to withdraw the warrant in the case. If he refuses to do so, Flemon will be turned over to the South Carolina authorities."[74]

They were banking on Governor Beaver to not go back on his word. But the Governor was still concerned about John's safety, and a curveball was thrown which changed the game entirely for the South Carolinians.

Governor Beaver wrote a telegram to Governor Richardson asking him to guarantee the safety of Mr. Yeldell. The response from the South Carolina Governor would determine Governor Beaver's final verdict. South Carolina did not see that coming. Of course, Governor Richardson had to respond in accordance with his request in order for Beaver to agree for John to be extradited from Pennsylvania. Beaver knew that he could not go back on his word. He also knew that if Yeldell got on a train with Strom and Lyons, he would never be seen alive again. Either way, he could lose the governorship in the next election year.

He realized the only way he could be governor again was to place the decision on Richardson. Richardson had to bring Yeldell back. If he didn't, come next election year, he would lose his job. This was a political poker game with incredibly high stakes for both governors. It was a genius move from Beaver. The telegram from Governor Beaver and the response from Governor Richardson follows below:

"Excerpts from HEARING THE FLEMON CASE.

The Colored Man Must Go South For Trial.

Promise of Safe Conduct.

Governor Beaver's Telegraph

After the hearing Governor Beaver sent this telegraph to Governor Richardson, but up to noon to-day no response had been received: "Colored and other Citizens fearful of violence to Yeldell. Will you kindly send thoroughly safe men to meet party at Augusta and afford safe conduct. Prisoner will leave Pittsburgh Thursday morning, if response is favorable."

Governor Richardson's Response

About 2 o'clock this afternoon the following response came from the Governor of South Carolina, addressed to Governor Beaver: "Your telegram received. I prefer that the prisoner should be brought to Columbia, and have so ordered agents. You can rest assured of the prisoner's safety. There is as little danger of violence in South Carolina as in any of her sister states North or South, and she only asks at their hands what she always readily grants to them – a strict and honest compliance with the constitution and laws of the Union."[75]

NO, HE DIDN'T! Did he just say that South Carolina abides by the Constitution and the laws of the Union?! Didn't I place a direct quote from Preston Brooks (one of South Carolina's favorite sons) saying words to the effect of advising South Carolinians to place the constitution underfoot, and step on it! I wasn't the only one feeling some kind of way when I read this. The Leavenworth Times of Leavenworth, Kansas couldn't believe it either.

"Excerpts from AN IMPUDENT: SOUTH CAROLINA CLAIM.

Richardson's dispatch is mere buncombe. South Carolina's "strict and honest compliance with the constitution and laws of the Union" has not been so marked as to arouse confidence in the message of her governor just quoted. If there is any one state more noted than any other defiance of the constitution and laws of the Union it is South Carolina. Her respect for the constitution was manifested by attempting nulification, and afterward by leading the secession movement. She was the first of all states to fire upon the flag of the union, and has never yet accepted in good faith the results of the war she precipitated. Her resistance to the laws of the United States conferring the suffrage on the negroes is as firm to-day as ever. Her soil has been enriched with the blood of thousands of freemen shot down in unprovoked massacres, or cowardly assassinated, simply because they sought to exercise the rights guaranteed to them by the constitution and laws of the United States. The republican form of government guaranteed by the Federal constitution has been suppressed in South Carolina. The state is ruled by an oligarchy, composed mainly of the old slave holders, the masses having been terrorized into subjection. Governor Richardson's message is an insult to the intelligence of the country."[76]

Governor Richardson may not have known it, but with his response to Governor Beaver, he had just placed South Carolina on trial. This was no longer about John Yeldell a.k.a Rev. E. F.

Flemon. From what I had been reading South Carolina had to give him a fair trial, better yet, he had to be found not guilty, any other verdict would have placed a blemish on the entire state.

John Travels to South Carolina

The time had come for John to make his way to South Carolina. His lawyers were already claiming victory, stating they had no doubt that he would be acquitted. The citizens of Pittsburgh seemed to be optimistic as well. John was to leave from the B&O railroad with two additional escorts apart from Marshals Lyon and Strom. The two officers, Detectives Fitzgerald and Dennison, were ordered to ride along to Cumberland, Maryland with the prisoner and the deputies. From Pennsylvania to Edgefield, John was to be always surrounded by law enforcement officers, his lawyers, or just people of color. There was a picture in the Pittsburgh Dispatch that showed the crowd of supporters and non-supporters. Sheriff Lyon and Marshall Strom were already on the train, but they would not have full custody of Yeldell/Flemon until they crossed the South Carolina state line. When the train pulled out of the station in Pennsylvania, a black woman ran behind the train shouting a prayer:

> "May the God of heaven strike this train from the track before it reaches the state line, is my prayer."
> 77

Why she would say that I have no idea. I guess her faith wasn't as strong as everyone else. The Governors of both Pennsylvania and South Carolina were in constant contact with each other throughout John's entire trip back to Edgefield. As Yeldell/Flemon's train entered each new state, his train was met by scores of African Americans showing their support, and wanting to shake his hand. When John reached Washington, D.C., the travelers had to wait for the next train south. This meant he had to be placed in lockup until the next scheduled train. People of color crowded around the Jailhouse just to get a glimpse of the now famous man. John was given the title of "the most talked of colored man in the land" by *the New York Times.*

While John was traveling to South Carolina, there were

several articles in southern papers that seemed to subconsciously warn, or at least remind South Carolinians, of how they should behave once John was there; as well as how he should be treated during the trial. An article in the Hartford Currant, which was a reprint of an earlier article published in a Charleston, South Carolina paper, stated:

> "In view of the notoriety which this (Flemon/Yeldell) case has attained, remarks the Charleston (S. C.) News and Courier, It is of the utmost importance to South Carolina that the law shall be complied with in the minutest particulars. In the eyes of the outside world – the world of political Pharisees – Edgefield county will sit at the bar with Yeldell and will be tried along with him. We are assured that the sentiment of that county generally is not hostile to him, and we believe that the people of Edgefield would be the first to protest against violence to him. The Blackwells and Jenningses and Talberts and Lyonses of Edgefield, we are sure would, if it were necessary, defend Yeldell with their lives."[78]

This was hilarious! This article, even at that time, was a crock. This article was published the day after John made it to Edgefield. It served as an undercover reminder to the families listed within it to stay away from John. There was another article that popped up in that search in *the Augusta Chronicle*

Excerpts from "Edgefield has bloodied past

By South Carolina Bureau Chief

Edgefield, S. C. – The clear-cut differences between the late Strom Thurmond and retiring U.S. Sen. Ernest "Fritz" Hollings echo the essence of the turbulent dynamic that has shaped South Carolina politics since colonial times.

Mr. Hollings, the tall, white-haired patrician with the rich, rumbling Lowcountry accent, epitomizes the power and pull of Charleston. In style, if not substance, he represents the heritage of the monied class of planters, bankers and merchants who founded the state and led it into the disastrous furnace of the Civil War.

Mr. Thurmond, with his scrappy vitality and legendary longevity, his military valor, his fiery defense of segregation and his nasal, Piedmont twang, inherited the raw political passion that challenged the Charleston elite and fueled the 1890s revolt of farmers and small town folk against the monied class.

J. Strom Thurmond was an Edgefield Man.

And in South Carolina, that means he was not only a cultural icon and a consummate political creature, but also a child of a notoriously violent place. It is a country where political arguments were often punctuated with a blast from a pistol or shotgun. So were many personal disputes – so many that Edgefield County, founded in 1785, was quickly branded "a dark and bloody ground."

Legend has it that every inch of the courthouse square – now dominated by Mr. Thurmond's statue and obelisk to the confederate dead – is stained by blood. The Edgefield District – a much larger jurisdiction than the current county – was a place far from the judges and courtrooms of Charleston. The people of the red, hilly land grew accustomed to settling grudges and disputes face-to-face, fist-to-fist, with duels and shootouts.

With its brawling reputation and unfiltered frontier heritage, the county also became a fertile field for South Carolina politicians noted for the violent defense of their ideals and adventurers willing to risk all for their own self-interest.

All are linked by traits forged in the battles fought against the Cherokee, the Yankee, the Lowcountry and one another, said Tonya Taylor, a historian and the director of the Tompkins Library in Edgefield, which serves as the home of the Old Edgefield District Genealogical Society.

"Hot-headedness and honor-bound," she said. "I've never seen such honor-bound people in my life. The same zeal you see in Strom Thurmond, you see in these men. That's what has driven Edgefield politics to be so bloody – the passion. They were so firm in their beliefs, they could not stand it if somebody thought otherwise."[79]

This article which was written in 2003. It goes on to describe the Edgefield people, mentioning many names that were written in this book, the book about my family. However, it could fit with the description you were reading for yourself in the 1880s. I understood it now. The article that was written in the News and Courier in Charleston was done as a definite warning, not as a reminder to the people of Edgefield. It was telling them that South Carolina was being closely watched and, just like you tell your children, it was best to just go and find somewhere and sit down. This is what this article was saying to them. Because the "monied class" of Charleston knew how the farm folk would normally react. This was getting better and better and I couldn't wait to get to the trial.

The Trial of John Yeldell a.k.a Rev. E.F. Flemon

Early on in this chapter, I compared this case to Dred Scott and Nat Turner. Were there cases today that could be compared to this? I realized that if this story was hidden away, exactly how many other stories up to today have been hidden as well. It is stories like these that will help us not to repeat history, and to move forward to a racist free life.

There was an additional article about the first set of Detectives, Fitzgerald, and Dennison. It seems that they did not get off where they were ordered to:

"THE OFFICERS SUSPENDED;

Detectives Fitzgerald and Dennison Laid Off for Disobedience

Detectives Fitzgerald and Dennison, who went with the Yeldell party as far as Washington, and who returned her Sunday evening were suspended from duty yesterday, by Inspector McAleese for disobedience of orders.

The Inspector gave the two men orders to accompany the deputies and their prisoner as far as Cumberland, Md., and then return home.

Upon arriving at Cumberland the two officers did not leave the train but proceeded to Washington. They were gone from Thursday to Sunday night it is stated that the Police Department suffered in consequence. When asked why they disobeyed orders the men stated that they thought a rescue might be attempted near Washington and accompanied the prisoner to that city. Upon returning home, they stopped on to meet some friends. A meeting will be held in the case within a few days and the men will be laid off for about two weeks."[80]

So, was it a rescue that was thwarted or an assassination? With all that you have read in this chapter so far, an assassination attempt can't be ruled out. It would have been a very convenient conclusion to an unsettling national news story. Nevertheless, John traveled on without further incident. He arrived in Edgefield on the 4th of August. By August 5th, Yeldell/Flemon was arraigned and he gave a plea of not guilty.

The trial was set to happen on August 9th. The friends of Yeldell had hired an additional lawyer, Col. John W. Echols, who was the prosecution during the extradition. He was hired because he was familiar with the case and the laws of South Carolina. John had two more lawyers as well, provided by Edgefield County: Arthur E. Tompkins, who had defended two other members of this same incident, and the very well-known and respected Honorable

W.C. Benet.

August 8th was the jury selection day and they selected a jury quickly. They picked the entire jury in one day, with the exception of one person. The twelfth person would be chosen before the trial in the morning. During the jury selection, however, Josh and Elijah Briggs, the two who claimed John fired the killing shot, had disappeared. The prosecution sent people out to find them. They were crucial to the case. As a matter of fact, they were the case. If they weren't found, John would definitely go free. It was rumored that a group of black men was trying to find them because they were testifying against Yeldell/Flemon. The papers blamed it on the Friends of Yeldell:

"A SCHEME THAT DIDN'T WORK

Friends of Yeldell Failed in an Attempt to Lynch the Briggs Boys

[SPECIAL TELEGRAM TO THE DISPATCH]

Columbia, S. C., August 9. – Josh and Lige Briggs are attracting more attention among the negroes than John Yeldell is. There were at least 1,000 negro men around the court house when court opened, and only about 500 could gain admission to the building. This afternoon, when court reassembled, the number of blacks had been increased 200 or 300.

The negroes are denouncing Josh and Lige Briggs for appearing to testify against Yeldell. It has been believed all along that this feeling against the Briggs, might assume a serious nature, and rumors this evening, which have been substantiated, have developed a plan among the negroes to get the two men out of the way, peaceably, if possible, or by lynching if necessary. Reliable information was conveyed to the proper parties this evening, that an attempt would be made by the negroes to inveigh Josh and Lige off to a certain negroe's house, three miles from town, and then and there assassinate

Comes to The Light

them. The purpose will now be defeated fort the friends of the men have taken them in charge and several bold, fearless and brave men will sit-up with them to-night, so that no harm may befall them.

The colored people in this vicenity have been quickly making up a purse for Yeldell, and it is understood that a meeting was held last night for the purpose of raising money for him. The public park in front of the court house is densely packed with negroes, and a large crowd of whites are on the street."[81]

The Briggs brothers were found before jury selection ended. However, the people of Edgefield were not that happy with the jury:

"THE JURY WITH FLEMON

The Edgefield Chronicle has a peculiar opinion of the jury drawn to serve at this term of the court in that county. In publishing the names of the jurors the Chronicle says:

This week we publish one of the petit juries for the August term, with the strong conviction, though we are sorry to express it, that the foulest and most red-handed murderer will be supremely safe in their hands, especially, if that murderer has money or influential friends. In truth, South Carolina juries have become another name for pitiful weakness and ignoble vascillation."[82]

I never did find the paper that gave the names, but the people of Edgefield felt the jury would not find him guilty. To be honest, I didn't think so either. Not because of the jury, but because of the mishap of the Governor, and the speed at which everything was happening. It was all going so fast. John was arrested on the 9th of July, with a trial date set for the 9th of August, which would be on a Friday. The trial began:

Excerpts from "YELDELL IN COURT.

Columbia S. C. August 9. – In the Edgefield Court, to-day, before the case of John Yeldell, alias Parson Flemon, was called for trial, ex-Governor Sheppard, of counsel for the prosecution, presented to the Court certificates from the Supreme Court of Georgia and Pennsylvania, showing that Colonel J. W. Echols of Pittsburgh, was a member of the bars of these respective States, and he was introduced to the Court by Mr. Sheppard, on whose motion and order was signed by Judge Pressley, allowing him to appear at the bar of this court.

The case of the State versus John Yeldell, indicted for murder, was the called. About this time the Blackwells came into the court with Josh and Lige Briggs, the principal witnesses for the state, Solicitor Nelson then stated that the prosecution was ready, but at the same time he desired to say to counsel on the other side, and especially to Colonel Echols, who was sent from Pittsburgh in the interest of Yeldell, that if the defense were not ready to go to trial, that the State would take pleasure in agreeing to a continuance." [83]

The continuance was requested because the witness for the defense was not available. However, the presiding Judge stated that a continuance would not be needed if they could use the testimony from the original trial had for Josh and Lige Briggs. The prosecution was fine with that, and they started to choose the Jurors:

Excerpts from "YELDELL IN COURT.

SECURING A JURY.

On the reassembling of court, the impaneling of the jury was entered upon. As the murder for which Yeldell stands indicted was committed before the enactment of the law cutting down the number of challenges in capital cases to ten, the Court ruled that the prisoner was entitled to 20.

In one hour's time the panel had been exhausted. The defense at this stage dad accepted 11 jurors, and objected to 20, and the State had exercised two objections both of which were colored men. The defense took two exceptions to the drawing of the jury. The first was in reference to a juror who had sat on the case when Josh and Lige Briggs were tried under the same indictment. The defense claimed he should stand aside for cause. The Court ruled that the juror was not disqualified. The other exception was noted when Mr. O. F. Cheatham was presented. He admitted that he had stated publicly, and to the solicitor, that he did not think Yeldell would be convicted. The Court ruled him incompetent to sit on the case.

THE DEFENSE EXCEPTED,

because the juror had not said that he thought the prisoner ought not to be convicted, but had only expressed the opinion that he would not be.

Two jurors were stood aside because they were related to the parties to the case. The State asked the Court to question Juror A. H. Smith as to whether he was opposed to capital punishment. Judge Pressley refused to do so, saying that he would not permit any citizen to say he was opposed to the law of the country.

The Jury Commissioner was called into the court room for the second time and drew five additional names. The State and the defense agreed to take the names of Messrs Allen and Hamilton, who were within calling distance of the court, put them in the box, and accept whichever one was drawn out. The name of J. K. Allen was drawn."[84]

This was actually funny because Mr. Allen refused and ran away. I guess he figured he didn't want any part of this. When they went to go and get Mr. Allen, he was sitting on a porch eating watermelon. He started running as soon as he saw the constable. The last time they saw him he was close to the county line. Since he did that, and it was so late in the day, the final juror would have to be chosen the next day.

The next day came after the weekend ended because the case started on a Friday. So, on Monday morning the final juror was chosen and the prosecution called their first witness. The Pittsburgh Dispatch gave a summary of the testimonies:

Excerpts from "YELDELL ACQUITTED.
THE TESTIMONY BROUGHT OUT.

> The following is a summary of the testimony adduced by the State: The attending physician testified as to the nature of the gunshot wounds which caused Blackwell's death. W. R. Parks testified that he was the trial justice who issued the warrant for Yeldell, Briggs and Harris for disturbing the peace and carrying concealed weapons, and that he appointed his brother, F. M. Parks as his constable to execute the warrant; and upon his report that he could not make the arrest by himself, he instructed his constable to get a sufficient number of men to assist him in making the arrest.
>
> F. M. Parks, the Constable, testified that he proceeded to make the arrest, but could not effect it without aid, and under instructions from the Trial Justice he summoned a posse of five men, among whom was James Blackwell. The posse left Parksville before day on the 30th of October, 1884, and proceeded to Josh Briggs' house, where Yeldell, Allen, Harris and Lige Briggs had taken refuge. Before reaching the house, the posse was fired into from ambush, and Blackwell was shot down."[85]

According to the papers, the prosecution's entire case was based on the testimony of Josh Briggs. "He testified that Yeldell, whom he recognized as the prisoner at the bar, was the man who killed Blackwell." He proceeded to give his version of the accounts of that day:

Excerpts from "YELDELL ACQUITTED.
RIGHT TO THE POINT

> John Yeldell, with other negroes, came to his house a little before sundown on the evening of the 29th of October, and stayed all night. Before daylight next morning Yeldell waked him up and said he heard a noise. They were expecting the white men, and went out in the lot. As Blackwell and a Mr. Stone were seen approaching Josh said "Halt" and immediately Yeldell fired and Blackwell fell. Then he (Josh) fired the second shot at the same parties near the gate. Josh was asked by the state whether any of the negroes in his party was hurt or hit by any bullets which were fired at them by the whites, and he replied that none of them were hurt." [86]

There was one more witness for the prosecution by the name of J. L. Stone. He was supposed to surround the house along with Blackwell. Mr. Stone testified that when he and Blackwell went to surround the house, he heard Josh say 'halt', and he recognized John Yeldell. At this the prosecution rest. I was confused because I didn't find one paper that stated the defense cross-examined the witness. I did find, however, that not only did they not cross-examine, the defense had no witness to call. This led straight to the summation of the lawyers. Both sides were given two hours for their closing. The prosecution went first, recalling the evidence and the case. Following this, the court broke for dinner. After dinner, the prosecution finished their closing and it switched to the defense. The defense went on for an hour ending its closing argument by saying it is:

> "not he but the state of South Carolina was on trial before the world."[87]

It was 6:00 pm when they handed everything over to the jury. During the waiting, it was rumored a threat was made to John's life if the verdict came back not guilty. It was because of that threat John's lawyers decided to keep him out of the courtroom for the verdict. The jury was ready three-and-a-half hours later. When the people heard of this, the courtroom filled immediately. Before the verdict was read, the Judge gave instructions to about 400 people in the court that there was to be no reaction to the verdict. An all-white jury came back with the verdict of not guilty:

Excerpts from "YELDELL ACQUITTED
SPEECHES OF THE LAWYERS

The charge of Judge Pressley was fair, but favorable to the prisoner on two important points. If the jury believed that they met at Josh Briggs' house, supposing there was a party on foot determined to lynch them or do any violence to them, the negroes assembled had a right to congregate together there and resist arrest, if possible, and if Blackwell had his gun presented at the time he was shot, then it was not murder for whoever killed him."[88]

According to the papers "on the first ballot 11 were for acquittal and 1 for conviction. It stood that way for every subsequent vote until 9:20 o'clock when the solitary juror who had been holding out for conviction went over to the majority."[89]

And there you have it John was acquitted. But was it really a fair trial? Is it fair when you make the area feel like they have no choice but to acquit? There was one article that seemed to be that way:

"Yeldell Acquitted.
By Telegraph to the Post-Dispatch.

Columbia, S. C., August 10 – The case against John Yeldell for the murder of Officer Blackwell was resumed to-day in Edgefield. The twelfth juror, who could not be procured yesterday, was quickly drawn and the evidence began. The prisoner had no witnesses. The State put up two negroes who have been closely connected with the case and were several years ago tried for the murder for which Yeldell was tried. The speech-making this afternoon and tonight was brief. The jury, a white one, found Yeldell "not guilty." This is the verdict the whites have expected. It was a settled thing under no circumstances would he receive a severe punishment. The negroes, however, were anticipating a verdict of guilty and they are rejoicing in Edgefield to-night. The trial was remarkably quick."[90]

This article bothered me. There was this one sentence that kept playing in my head, "This is the verdict the whites have expected." What did they mean by that? I wasn't sure until I found this next article. This next article supported all of my bad feelings that I began to have when Echols became John's lawyer. The article was very short and to the point:

"Rev. Flemon Acquitted.

Edgefield, S. C., Aug 13 – The trial of John Yeldell, alias Rev. Flemon, colored, of Pittsburgh, for the murder of James S. Blackwell, in October, 1884, ended in his acquittal."[91]

There seemed to be no issues on the surface. Yet, when you are the researcher, you find a problem. Although this article is dated August 13th, it was posted in a paper that was dated August 8th. The verdict was not given until August 13th. How did they know that on the 8th of August the jury would come back with a not guilty verdict on August 13th? I realized then that this was a setup. Even if John could be found guilty, he was never going to be. What made matters worse was the next article that I found:

"Morning Tribune

John Yeldell, alias Rev. E. F. Flemon, the negro who was recently surrendered to South Carolina by the Governor of Pennsylvania, has been acquitted. He was of a party of negroes who resisted a lynching party and the court instructed the jury that he had a lawful right to defend himself. This charge and the knowledge that the whole country was watching the progress of the trial led to his acquittal. He was provided with a military escort and conveyed to Columbia, where, it is believed, he is safe. The results of this trial shows that even South Carolina is progressing and it is not necessary to inquire too curiously into the reasons which brought the freeing of Yeldell."[92]

This was a sarcastically written article. I was totally disappointed because I agreed with the sarcasm of this article. With all the work that was done, it all went to waste. I was really hoping he would get a fair trial. Did I think he did it? Yes! But I believe it was self-defense. I feel the case was poorly done on both sides. With the articles above, I think it was safe to say I was not alone. One thing I did know was this is why this story was kept out of our history books. It showed the shady side of politics.

The objective now was to get John safely out of South Carolina. There were threats to his life while he was in jail awaiting travel to leave. The family of the Blackwells threatened John's life as well. Press Blackwell, the victim's father, stated that as long as he (John) was with the sheriff (Outzs), he would not harm him. However, as soon as John was out of Outzs' custody, that Blackwell would kill him. The same way John came into South Carolina is the same way he left; with a police escort, almost all the way home. It took thirty-two days from beginning to end.

Rev. Flemon went on to live his life in Pennsylvania. He eventually moved to Sharon, Pennsylvania, probably because, in Pittsburgh, he was always referred to as the man who escaped being hung.

Chapter 12 – The True Accounts of the Rev. Elijah F. Flemon

There was one more story I needed to share. That story was John's, or who we now know as Elijah. Reverend Flemon spoke in front of a small audience at a church in Akron, Ohio on 5 November 1890. The story is rather long, but it was the first time he spoke publicly about his life and the incident itself.

"A THRILLING ESCAPE

HUNTED BY MEN ARMED WITH WINICHESTERS

JOHN YELDELL RELATES A STARTLING STORY OF PERSECUTION – HE TELLS WHY HE IS A REPUBLICAN.

From Saturday's Daily Beacon

John Yeldell, alias "Rev. E. F. Flemon," delivered an interesting lecture to a small audience at the Zion A. M. E. Church last evening. Rev. Flemon is a resident of Ravenna and has some very interesting experiences, which he narrated last evening in a telling way. He is very much in earnest in regard to the advancement of the race to which he belongs, and the story of his travels in the South as a boy and a man, his trial at Edgefield, S. C., for the murder of deputy Sheriff James Blockwell and his subsequent acquittal illustrate forcibly a sad feature of Southern life.

Rev. Flemon was introduced by Rev. Geo. Cliff and spoke substantially as follows:

I was born of slave parents in 1860. When freedom came my parents still worked for the old master. As my father died in my early boyhood and left my mother with three children, I got but little education. When I was nearly in my teens my mother remarried and my new father, though he did his best for us, did not think education a necessity. My early life was spent in the hardest of rough work and when about 15 years of age, during the Hayes campaign, I caught my first glimpse of negro terrorism.

Negroes are Republicans. Only one in a hundred will vote the Democratic ticket, and we believe that this one should be banished from America. That November morning, Mr. Nobles, a friend of mine, walked to Edgefield to cast his ballot. As he stepped down he brushed against a white man, who stabbed him. Mr. Lyons cried out that a "nigger" had hit a white man. The white men rushed for their guns, for negroes were not allow to go armed. Mr. Nobles started to run but was shot dead in his tracks. He was shot by Mr. Lyons, and Mr. Lyons, when he came north to seize my body, did not deny the fact. Was he arrested and punished? No. It was but a dead "nigger." Do you believe in seeing your race shot down? I am a minister, but one who would rather be killed than see any people so downtrodden.

Shortly after this a man and his wife were found dead in a strip of woods. It must be a "nigger," a white man would not do such a thing. Six negroes were found, two of them preachers, and without charge or trial they were shot down in their chains. In their chains they were buried, and if a bone is left to-day it is still in chains. This is why I am out of the South today. A friend of mine, a Mr. McKnight, was sent to that part of the State to preach the gospel. He was in a voting place and was asked in a persuasive tone if he did not want to vote a certain ticket. He left through the window taking the sash with him and ran five miles before he stopped. He left, feeling that God had not called him to preach in that section.

On the day of Garfield's election I was but 19 years of age, and, although not a voter myself, I controlled 165 votes. As we came near the voting place, the rear guard of our men was attacked by well-known Southerners with clubs and stones. I told my men to stand firm. Mr. Lyons drove up and I caught his horse by the bridle, asking him what he wanted. He wanted the negroes to go from the polls. I refused and inside of four weeks I was forced to leave the State, for 25 men were hunting me, with the avowed purpose of killing me. But not a negro vote was counted at that election. Is that a consolidated South? A large portion of the citizens and tax-payers have no voice in government. Some negroes sing, "Take all this world, and give me Jesus." I want Jesus but I want my share of the world also.

After two years' banishment I returned to South Carolina to a place called Dark Corner. This is the place where it was stated that I pushed ladies of the sidewalk. Four men and three children composed the city, so that the absurdity of the story appears on it face. I went back to my old home, because I wanted to talk for Blaine, and for 18 months I staid, and in that time I carried on a Blaine campaign, and the Democrats knew nothing of that fact. During the day I run the engine, picked cotton and hoed corn and they knew no more of me. One day I was walking down the road when John Parks rode up to me and asked me what the shooting in the woods the night before meant. I told him I did not know, and he with a crowd at his back demanded that I be searched for a pistol. What right had he to investigate such matters? But no! I showed the pistol to him and his friends and dared them to take it. He had a crowd with him; with me I had but three boys, all of whom are to-day sleeping under the sod, because they would not take their own parts. Park and his friends, cowards that they were, retired and recruited to 25 – marshals, deputies and sheriffs are easily made in that state when a "nigger" is to be hunted down – and when I passed them again, five shots were fired at me, two passing through my hat. They followed us through the woods all night. The next day 10 sheriffs came for me with 10 warrants over their shoulders, warrants which would speak 16 times. I was working in the cotton field at the time and concluded I better run. I landed on the other side of the woods before they did and as I ran through my cabin, I seized my rifle and cartridges, reached the woods and climbed into a ditch. By night 16 sheriffs were at hand; they rode for me all night, but they rode in vain. Friday morning as were in the house of a negro, six in all, we heard them coming. We got out into a shed and waited for them. They stopped in front of the shed and made their plans to surround us. One of our men commanded them to halt, upon which they opened fire. We did likewise, though the odds were strongly against us. Two of these sheriffs were carried away dead. After incredible hardships, I found my way North. – The rest of my story is well known – carried South, tried and honorably acquitted. The night of my acquittal the jail yard was surrounded by hundreds of blood-thirsty men seeking my life. But through the influence of the Northern States on public sentiment I was brought home in a special car with great care and trouble. I will never return to the South. I have had enough.

You say that you are all right. You place me in charge of affairs who will not even look at you. You must see your own race advanced. When you graduate, you are content to clean someone's horse or serve at someone's table. You are afraid to push yourselves. Why are you brethren in the South so treated? Because they are Republicans. I am a Republican from head to foot. Not a colored man should vote a Democratic ticket. Whatever has been done for the negro has been done by the Republican party. If a Democrat should ask me to vote for him I would be tempted to kick him down stairs. We are divided. We must stand as a unit or our future is indeed dark."[93]

Politics is a huge part of my family and the strong convictions in John's choice to be a Republican or to not be afraid to say his choice was natural. But you have to wonder, would he feel the same way today? The Republican party that John believed in was the party of Abraham Lincoln. John couldn't understand how any person of color could be a Democrat because Democrats did nothing to help "Negroes." The Republican party of today is NOT the Republican party of that time. Would he have switched? There were pieces of most of the stories that I shared in this book you could find in the stories that have happened today.

Learning about John gave me an insight into why it has been so hard to find my Yeldell family. John was continuously picked on by Mr. Lyons until he finally left Edgefield. Given the attitude of how the Edgefield men were like when they couldn't get to John, his family became fair game. This stopped them from keeping in touch, because, like the story said they found John through letters that were sent and received; if you couldn't come to visit, we wouldn't talk at all.

My grandfather traveled to Pennsylvania and his family traveled to DC. He could have been going to see John when he visited his sister. Their forced secrecy is what broke this family up. I pray that I can piece it back together. Rev. Flemon was 82 years old when he died and he took his new name to his death. When his son completed his death certificate, the names of his parents were not listed. He was married twice and had five children. As I continue to follow his tree I am learning that his family just may have died out, however, the research is still ongoing for that.

Figure 21 - Calling All Branches Logo,
Created by Johnny Sajem

Chapter 13 – Calling All Branches

Researching my roots, as you have seen, has taken me through some ups and downs. Although I have shared some of the highlights from my research results with you, the work is a continuing process. With all of the information, I have found, my ultimate goal has always been to connect the white families to the black families; to address the racial tension head-on by teaching people that hating people simply because of the color of their skin meant they hated members of their own family. With the finding of Moses and his 45 children, I was definitely on the right track. For every black family that I found I was able to connect them with our white family. The goal now was to bring them together. But how do I bring white and black families together when they don't know each other.

It was at that point that I had come back in contact with a Yeldell I had met during my early years of researching. Her name was Opal Mitchell Lee. Opal's family connected to the white Yeldell's whose family moved from Edgefield to Texas. Although I haven't been able to connect her branch of the Yeldell family to mine, she has always been a trusted and most loved resource and mentor. Opal reminded me of my Uncle Rob because of her political and grassroots works throughout her community.

She was one of the first people that I sent letters to simply because we shared the same family name. In the 1960s and 1970s. She was a dedicated civil rights activist from Texas to California. Our first correspondence with each other was her response to my letter. In and amongst the other items she shared with me, was an update about a class action suit that had been filed against a large oil company for stealing land from the African American children who were born to her grandfather, Starling Yeldell, who was a white man. Her goal was to get as many African American Yeldell's to sign this petition so that the lawsuit to retrieve the land could move forward. She didn't achieve enough signatures to accomplish this goal. However, Opal became the black Erin Brockovich of our time by becoming involved with cases similar to the Yeldell case.

Figure 22 - Mrs. Opal Mitchell Lee, Photo courtesy of Myrtle Green

Opal helped with cases for people who couldn't help themselves. She was so good at what she did that the historically black college, Texas Southern University's Earl Carl Institute Center for Civil Advocacy (CCA), named a grant program after her, calling it the Opal Mitchell Lee Property Preservation Project Grant. This grant was created to address the legal challenges lower-income people face in maintaining their real property and enhancing their wealth.[94] As I learned more about Opal I realized that she was a living black history fact.

I am sure some of you have heard of the Sixth-Floor Museum at Dealey Plaza in Dallas, TX. This museum chronicles the assassination and legacy of President John F. Kennedy; interprets the Dealey Plaza National Historic Landmark District and the John F. Kennedy Memorial Plaza.[95] There is an exhibit in the museum called the Oral History Project. This project explores the history & culture of the 1960s. These interviews offer personal insights into the life, death, and legacy of President John F. Kennedy.[96] In June 2011 she was recorded saying where she was and what she was doing during that tragic day. Opal was interviewed because of what she did to help African Americans. She was considered a known civil rights activist; a living legend.

Opal had become sick with a terminal illness, but she wanted to see her family together. Her daughter Myrtle was planning to bring Opal to Washington, DC for the opening of the newly built Smithsonian African American Museum. This was important because the research that Opal did for her family and the help she provided to so many others had landed her book in that museum. It was at that point the idea was given that when she comes here for the opening we have the reunion at the same time. Myrtle asked me if I would spearhead this event. I was more than happy to do this. I posted on Facebook the following message:

"CALLING ALL BRANCHES!!!!
THE WAIT IS FINALLY OVER!!!

Someone has decided to take on the task of planning the next family reunion for ALL branches of our family. This reunion includes: Adams, Bugg, Bush, Borum, Dansby, Gilchrist, Harling, Harrison, Hightowers, Higgins, Holloways, Matthews/Mathis, Palmore, Peterson, Quarles, Ryans, Senior, Settles, Sheffey, Smith, Talbert, Weaver, Williams, Yeldell, Young and many more.

The coordinator is Myrtle Green of Duncanville, TX and she is the daughter of Opal Lee. They descend from a man named Starling Yeldell. Opal is a well-known activist in Corsicana, Texas. I met Opal via snail mail. I sent her a letter asking her about her Yeldell connection. She responded by letting me know about a class action suit to gather as many Yeldell's because the Shell gas company had stolen the rights of the land from the black children of Starling. Although she didn't win the suit it was equivalent to Erin Brockovich. She has taken on several other projects in her life and because of her actions will be in the African

American Museum. Myrtle thought that in lieu of her mom being honored like this and the last year of our first African American President being in office this would be the perfect time to have a reunion in DC with all of the branches.

This is a huge task and one that I am definitely willing to help with. The goal is for the reunion to be held here in Washington, DC around the grand opening of the African American Museum. This will open in the Fall of 2016. A tentative schedule of activities are as follows:

The 2016 Calling All Branches Family Reunion will include:

- The opening ceremony for the Smithsonian African-American Museum and tour
- Tour of the White House
- Tour of the Capital and Supreme Court and more

This has the potential of becoming one of the largest events in DC that do not have a celebrity or politician attached to the planning. If you are interested in being a part of this wondrous event, please let me ("me" being the representative passing the information on) know. Hotels and park location searches have already started."

This message brought close to thirty family members from 8 different family names to the first planning meeting for this reunion. We were moving along well until interest started to drop and the number of people attending the meetings started to dwindle. It was at that point we knew who was serious about this and who wasn't. With the small numbers in attendance, we needed to do something that would bring interest back to the reunion so I created an invite on Facebook that said the following:

"John 17:22 And the glory which thou gavest me I have given them; that they may be one, even as we are one:

> After the Civil War our ancestors left where they lived in search of families lost. Whether they were taken away or sold away, they were now lost. Great measures were taken to find these lost souls. Ads were placed in newspapers, magazines and read on church pulpits trying to find Moms and Dads, Sisters and Brothers.
>
> In our ancestor's death, they still search for their lost families. How do they do it through their descendants? We call them family historians and genealogist. This is a rare opportunity for us. The people that I work with are heeding the call of our ancestors and finding their lost families and those families are *YOU*.
>
> I know that other reunions will happen at this time, but please consider joining us this one year, this one time. Help bring rest to our ancestor. Let us meet and rejoice as we celebrate LIFE, FAMILY & LOVE.
>
> Calling All Branches Family Reunion
> September 2-4, 2016
> At the National Harbor in Ft. Washington, MD"

This message made our Facebook group page grow to over 1100 members before the reunion. Our registrations soared and people were excited again. Marketing to our different families, both white and black played a huge part in the forming of this reunion. We advertised in places like Facebook, Twitter, Instagram and more. Our goal was to make every family a part of this huge event being as though this would be the first time this family would have been together like this for over 200 hundred years. My cousin Brian had created an advertisement that was so profound it brought attention from two known newspapers in South Carolina.

Since I was the overall coordinator of this event, I was

interviewed by the Index-Journal of Greenwood, South Carolina and the Post and Courier of Charleston, South Carolina. Both papers shared the importance of this reunion and how bringing the families together both black and white would start a healing process between races one family at a time. ***The Index-Journal*** reporter went one step further and spoke with a woman name Sonya Calhoun. She learned about the reunion through word of mouth and said:

Excerpts from Branches of the Same Tree: A Family Reunion for the History Books

"I found out people I had known for years were family."[97]

On Labor Day weekend September 2016, this event brought together the families of 45 different surnames out of over 190. Several branches of our family tree had come together for the first time since the early 1800s. The main events for each day during that weekend was a meet and greet, a family cookout, a prayer breakfast and finally a dinner. At the dinner, we honored our Ancestors by setting a plate on the table for them.

This reunion was just what the ancestors planned it to be. It was the start of a new idea, the beginning of the families coming together as one. Right after the prayer breakfast, the idea was introduced to have a different family plan the reunion every other year. As soon as the idea was spoken we had two families to step up for the reunion years 2018 and 2020. The Bugg Family would plan for 2018, while the Hightower/Little/Bush family took the reins for 2020. I never thought that being interested in the size of one family would turn into experiencing such life-changing events.

Figure 23 - The First Congregation for Springfield Baptist of D.C., Photo taken by Addison Scurlock Photography

Chapter 14 – Honoring the Ancestors

I often wonder with all that has occurred is there anything more that I can do to continue the growth of our families. My ongoing research includes getting more families tested in the hopes that we match each other via DNA. My mother was tested with three different DNA companies and with one company alone, she has over 1000 DNA relatives. Several of those cousins carry the same surnames as my mother. It is a part of the reason the Calling All Branches Family Reunion was created. My goal now is to teach this, share this and hope to inspire others to do the same. DNA doesn't lie and through it we have connected 197 surnames, all coming from or having ties to the Edgefield County area. This book is my legacy that I am leaving to my children as well as the entire family. It is an oral and now documented history of who we are and where we come from. I end this book by honoring our Ancestors listing every one of their names. Bringing them back to life through every person that reads their names.

The Families of Edgefield, South Carolina

Abocho, Adams, Abney, Alexander, Alford, Allen, Anderson, Andrews, Armstead, Baptiste/Baptist/Batiste, Benefield/Bennafield, Bedell, Berry, Bettis, Blalock, Bland, Blocker, Bonham, Borum, Bosket, Bowie, Bowles, Brighthop/Brighthart, Broadwater, Brooks, Brunson, Bugg/Buggs/Briggs, Brown, Burris, Burt, Burton, Bush, Butler, Calhoun, Campbell, Carley/Corley, Carroll, Carter, Clark, Chambers, Chappelle, Collier, Collins, Coleman, Cooke/Cook, Cummings, Daniel, Dansby, Davis, Demery/Dimery, Devore/Devoe/Deveaux, Dobey, Donaldson, Dorn, Dozier, Duncan, Ellington, Etheridge/Etheredge, Evans, Fair, Felder, Fitzgerald, Fitzpatrick, Frazier, Freeman, Garrett, Garrison, Gaskins, Gibson, Gilchrist, Gilliam, Glass, Glover, Goins/Goines, Gomillion, Goodwin, Gordon, Gould, Gray/Grey, Greene, Griffin, Hamilton, Hammond, Harling, Harris, Harrison, Hatcher, Henderson, Hightower/Hytower/Hightour, Higgins, Hill, Hobbs, Holloway, Holmes, Hubbard, Jackson, Jennings, Jeter, Johnson, Jones, Keesee/Kizzee, Kemp, Key, Laborde, Lagroon, Lake, Lanham, Lewis, Little, Lucas, Manderville, Martin, Matthews/Mathis, Mays/Mayes, McCain/McKane, McCall, McCollum, McKie, McKinley, Medlock, Meriwether/Merriwether/Merriweather, Miles, Miller, Mims, Moore, Moss, Oliphant, Oliver, Ouzts, Pace, Palmore, Parker, Parrish, Perry, Peterson, Phillips, Philpot, Pinckney/Pinkney, Portee, Powell, Pullen, Price, Quarles, Ramsey, Reed /Reid/ Ready, Richardson, Robinson, Roney/Rooney, Roundtree Russell, Ryan/Ryans, Samuels, Scruggs, Scurry, Senior, Sellers, Settles, Sharpton, Sheffey, Shibley/Shivers, Simkins/Simpkins, Sheppard, Smith, Sparrow, Speaks, Stalworth/Stallworth, Stephens/Stevens, Sullivan, Swearingen/Swingarn, Talbert/Tolbert, Timmerman, Thompson, Thurmond, Tresevant, Truesdale, Tucker, Turner, Tyler, Walker, Wallace, Waller, Ware, Washington, Watson, Weaver/Wever, West, Witcher, White, Wigfall, Williams, Wilson, Wise, Womack, Wrights, Yeldell, Young

Figure 24 - Donya Williams Photo taken by Donya Williams

ABOUT THE AUTHOR

For more than 20 years Donya Williams has researched her roots out of Edgefield, South Carolina. As she researched her family there came a time where sharing her findings was a must and she did so through a blog on WordPress that was followed by family members, other researchers, and friends. As her knowledge of the Genealogical field grew so did her need to expose others to what she had learned. Donya became the administrator of two genealogical Facebook groups and created a Facebook page that would share the information she found through research with others.

After years of finding and connecting her family to each other the stories from her blog and much more have been compiled and told in a way that only Donya can do in the new book

Comes to The Light:
Learning About the Entangled Families of Edgefield, South Carolina

Donya is a single mother of four children, one of which is an autistic graduating senior in Maryland. She continues her research while taking care of her mother and children.

Photo Credits
Figure 1 - Poem and Photo Submitted by S. Alexander
Figure 2 – Town of Edgefield Entrance, taken by Julian Hunter Pendarvis, 15 July 2017
Figure 3 – Springfield Baptist of Edgefield Cemetery, Photo taken by Donya Williams
Figure 4 – Lula Yeldell Robertson, Photo courtesy of Jennelle Yeldell Turner
Figure 5 - Jefferson and Annie Mae Yeldell, Photo taken by Addison Scurlock Photography
Figure 6 - Springfield Baptist of DC, Photo taken by Charles Cooke
Figure 7 - Jefferson Davis Yeldell, Photo taken by Addison Scurlock Photography
Figure 8 - Robert Lee Yeldell Photo courtesy of Juanita Yeldell-Williams
Figure 9 - Yeldell Towers, Photowas taken by Donya Williams
Figure 10 - Snapshot of 1900 U.S. Federal Census, Snapshot was taken by Donya Williams courtesy of NARA
Figure 11 - Annie Mae Senior-Yeldell, Photo taken by Addison Scurlock Photography
Figure 12 - Snapshot of Whitfield Brooks Will, Snapshot was taken by Donya Williams courtesy of NARA
Figure 13 - Southern Chivalry Argument versus Club's Photo credit New York Public Library Creator John L. Magee
Figure 14 - One-hundred and thirty-nine-year-old Bible, Photo taken by Donya Williams
Figure 15 - Mama Lula's House, Photo was taken by Donya Williams
Figure 16 - Mama Lula's Barn, Photo was taken by Donya Williams
Figure 17 - Lula "Mama Lula" Peterson-Senior, Photo Courtesy of Juanita Yeldell-Williams
Figure 18 - Senior Family Women, Photos courtesy of James Ryan and Juanita Yeldell-Williams, Collage by Donya Williams
Figure 19 - Deputy Lyon, Photo courtesy of The Pittsburgh Press c. 1889
Figure 20 - Deputy Strom, Photo courtesy of The Pittsburgh Press c. 1889
Figure 21 - Calling All Branches Logo, Created by Johnny Sajem
Figure 22 - Mrs. Opal Mitchell Lee, Photo courtesy of Myrtle Green
Figure 23 - The First Congregation for Springfield Baptist of D.C., Photo taken by Addison Scurlock Photography
Figure 24 - Donya Williams Photo was taken by Donya Williams

---

[1] Revolvy, https://www.revolvy.com/main/index.php?s=Lords%20Proprietor. Accessed 26 July 2017
[2] Revolvy, https://www.revolvy.com/main/index.php?s=Lords%20Proprietor. Accessed 26 July 2017
[3] The Great Migration 1915-1960 http://www.blackpast.org/aah/great-migration-1915-1960

[4] 1900 U.S. Census, Blocker, Edgefield, South Carolina, ; Roll: 1526; Page: 13A; Enumeration District: 0110; FHL microfilm: 1241526 Ancestry.com (http://www.ancestry.com : accessed 1996)
[5] http://www.angeltherapy.com/blog/3-types-angels-are-you Accessed 16 September 2014
[6] The Free Dictionary by Farlex http://www.thefreedictionary.com/ancestor Accessed 7 December 2013
[7] Infamous Lynchings http://www.americanlynching.com/infamous-old.html#billington
[8] Lynching, Whites and Negroes, 1882 – 1968 http://archive.tuskegee.edu/archive/bitstream/handle/123456789/511/Lyching%201882%201968.pdf?sequence=1&isAllowed=y
[9] Lynching, Whites and Negroes, 1882 – 1968 http://archive.tuskegee.edu/archive/bitstream/handle/123456789/511/Lyching%201882%201968.pdf?sequence=1&isAllowed=y
[10] Statehouse Report, "New Report says 164 lynched in Jim Crow S.C." http://www.statehousereport.com/2015/02/12/164-lynched-in-jim-crow-s-c-report-says/
[11] The Chicago Defender, http://www.blackpast.org/aah/chicago-defender-1905
[12] Gloria R. Lucas, Slave Records of Edgefield County, South Carolina. (Edgefield County Historical Society, Edgefield County, South Carolina, 2010), p. 55-56
[13] Robert W. Fogel and Stanley L. Engerman, Time on the Cross: The Economics of American Negro Slaves (W. W. Norton and Company, Inc. 1989)
[14] Robert W. Fogel and Stanley L. Engerman, Time on the Cross: The Economics of American Negro Slaves (W. W. Norton and Company, Inc. 1989)
[15] National Humanities Center Resource Toolbox. The Making of African American Identity, Vol. I, 1500-1865.
[16] "The Price of a Human Being," South Carolina's Information Highway, http://www.sciway.net/afam/slavery/flesh.html#auction. Accessed 9 November 2013
[17] "The Price of a Human Being," South Carolina's Information Highway, http://www.sciway.net/afam/slavery/flesh.html#auction. Accessed 9 November 2013
[18] Ibid
[19] Miscellaneous Probate Records, 1785-1868; Indexes to Records, 1785-1957; Author: South Carolina. Probate Court (Edgefield County); Probate Place: Edgefield, South Carolina
[20] The Last Will and Testament of Whitfield Brooks
[21] http://www.blackpast.org/about-us accessed March 2013
[22] http://www.blackpast.org/about-us accessed March 2013
[23] The Statutes at Large; Being a Collection of all the Laws of Virginia, volume 2 (1823) by William W. Henning
[24] Octavia V. Rogers Albert, *The House of Bondage*, (Hunt & Eaton 1890) p. 1

[25] "South Carolina Duels," The Evening Star, Washington, DC 11 Jan 1889, Retrieved 25 April 2017
[26] Ibid.
[27] "South Carolina Duels," The Evening Star, Washington, DC 11 Jan 1889, Retrieved 25 April 2017
[28] Sydney Nathan, To Free a Family: The Journey of Mary Walker. (Presidents and Fellows of Harvard College, 2012), p. 107.
[29] Charles Sumner, "The Crime Against Kansas: The Apologies for the Crime, The True Remedy." Speech of Hon. Charles Sumner in the Senate of the United States, May 19 and 20, 1856. Cornell University Libraries
[30] "The Kansas-Nebraska Act," U.S. Online History Textbook, http://www.ushistory.org/us/31a.asp. Accessed 7 August 2013.
[31] World Heritage Encyclopedia, http://www.ebooklibrary.org/articles/eng/Preston_Brooks, accessed, 27 February 2017
[32] "Canefight! Preston Brooks and Charles Sumner" U.S. History, http://www.ushistory.org/us/31e.asp Accessed 9 August 2017
[33] Holt Merchant, South Carolina Fire-Eater: The Life of Laurence Massillion Keitt, 1824-1864, University of South Carolina Press 1 July 2014
[34] William E. Gienapp, the Origins of the Republican Party, Oxford University Press, 4 June 1987.
[35] Ibid.
[36] Anti-slavery bugle. (New-Lisbon, Ohio), 01 Nov. 1856. Chronicling America: Historic American Newspapers. Lib. of Congress. <http://chroniclingamerica.loc.gov/lccn/sn83035487/1856-11-01/ed-1/seq-1/> Accessed January 25, 2014
[37] Causes of Death in the Late 19th Century, http://www.hctgs.org/deathcertificates/causes_of_death.htm. Accessed 25 April 2017
[38] Yorkville Enquirer, 05 Feb 1857. Chronicling America: Historic American Newspapers. Lib. Of Congress, http://chroniclingamerica.loc.gov/lccn/sn84026925/1857-02-05/ed-1/seq-2/#date1=1789&sort=relevance&rows=20&words=BROOKS+Brooks+death+Death+DEATH+Preston+PRESTON&searchType=basic&sequence=0&index=5&state=&date2=1924&proxtext=preston+brooks+death&y=9&x=17&dateFilterType=yearRange&page=2 accessed 2/28/2017
[39] The Daily Dispatch (Richmond Va.) 1850-1884, http://chroniclingamerica.loc.gov/lccn/sn84024738/1857-02-04/ed-1/seq-2/#date1=1789&index=6&rows=20&words=Brooks+death+Preston&searchType=basic&sequence=0&sort=date&state=&date2=1924&proxtext=preston+brooks+death&y=9&x=17&dateFilterType=yearRange&page=1 accessed 2/28/2017
[40] Old Edgefield District Genealogical Society, Edgefield County S,C African American Cemeteries Vol. 1 pg 67-72

[41] Ibid.

[42] *National Treasure.*,Dir. Jon Turtletaub, Walt Disney Studios Motion Pictures, 19 November 2004, Film

[43] Edgefield South Carolina, Calendar of Events, http://www.exploreedgefield.com/event/southern-studies-showcase-3 accessed: 03/07/2017

[44] Charleston Where History Lives, http://www.africanamericancharleston.com/lowcountry.html accessed March 7, 2017

[45] National Conference of State Legislature, http://www.ncsl.org/research/human-services/state-laws-regarding-marriages-between-first-cousi.aspx, Accessed 2 June 2016

[46] Medicinenet.com. Medical Definition of Pellagra, http://www.medicinenet.com/script/main/art.asp?articlekey=4821. Accessed 12 August 2017

[47] Medicinenet.com. Medical Definition of Pellagra, http://www.medicinenet.com/script/main/art.asp?articlekey=4821. Accessed 12 August 2017

[48] American History USA, https://www.americanhistoryusa.com/topic/indentured-servant/ Accessed June 3, 2016

[49] PBS History Detective Special Investigations http://www.pbs.org/opb/historydetectives/feature/indentured-servants-in-the-us/

[50] PBS History Detective Special Investigations http://www.pbs.org/opb/historydetectives/feature/indentured-servants-in-the-us/

[51] E.Z.F. (1922 August 3) Quintuplets and More, Negro Farmer has 45 Children, The Charlotte Observer (Charlotte, North Carolina). Retrieved from https://www.newspapers.com

[52] Obituary Notes, (1884 Oct 22) taken from Charleston Courier, Weekly Raleigh Register, https://www.newspapers.com/image/?spot=9545228

[53]

[54] Ibid

[55]

[56] Newspapers.com retrieved 2015-2017, www.newspapers.com

[57] "A FULL AND TRUE ACCOUNT OF THE EDGEFIELD TROUBLE "A correct statement of the Killing of the Constable Blackwell by a gang of Negro desperados – No further trouble Anticipated." The Abbeville Press and Banner, Abbeville, South Carolina November 5, 1884 retrieved, April 5, 2017

[58] "The Parksville Tragedy", The Watchman and Southron, Sumter, South Carolina, 11 November 1884. Accessed 21 August 2017

[59] "Serious and sad", The Weekly Advertiser, Montgomery, AL, 11 November 1884, retrieved 10 April 2017

[60] "Black Codes", http://www.history.com/topics/black-history/black-codes, Accessed 10 April 2017

[61] "ACCUSED OF MURDER" The Buffalo Commercial, Buffalo, N.Y. retrieved 10 April 2017
[62] "Something About Yeldell", Abbeville Press and Banner, 17 July 1889
[63] "FLEMON MUST BE HELD", Pittsburgh Dispatch, Pittsburgh, PA. July 12, 1889. Retrieved April 11, 2017
[64] "PARSON FLEMON'S STORY", The New York Times, New York, NY 29 July 1889, retrieved April 11, 2017
[65] "OUT FOR AN AIRING", Pittsburgh Dispatch, Pittsburgh, PA 14 July 1889 retrieved April 11, 2017
[66] "WILL STAND BY FLEMON", Pittsburgh Daily Post, Pittsburgh. PA 16 July 1889. Retrieved 12 April 2017
[67] "FLEMON BADLY IS WANTED", Pittsburgh Daily Post, Pittsburgh. PA 15 July 1889. Retrieved 13 April 2017
[68] "The Most Talked of Colored Man in the Land" The New York Times, 29 July 1889
[69] "FLEMON IS YELDELL", In the Congressman's office, Pittsburgh Dispatch, Pittsburgh, PA 20 July 1889. Retrieved 14 April 2017
[70] FLEMON IS YELDELL", In the Congressman's office, Pittsburgh Dispatch, Pittsburgh, PA 20 July 1889. Retrieved 14 April 2017
[71] FLEMON IS YELDELL", In the Congressman's office, Pittsburgh Dispatch, Pittsburgh, PA 20 July 1889. Retrieved 14 April 2017
[72]
[73] "YELDELL IN SOUTH CAROLINA", The Abbeville Press and Banner, Abbeville, S. C. 07 August 1889. Retrieved 14 April 2017
[74] "YELDELL WILL COME BACK", The Manning Times, Manning, South Carolina, 31 July 1889. Retrieved 14 April 2017
[75] "HEARING THE FLEMON CASE." Harrisburg Telegraph, Harrisburg, Pennsylvania, 31 July 1889. Retrieved 14 April 2017
[76] "AN IMPUDENT: SOUTH CAROLINA CLAIM", The Leavenworth Times, Leavenworth, Kansas 07 August 1889. Retrieved. 14 April 2017
[77] "Rev. E.F. Flemmon, Murderer and Perjurer, Reluntantly Takes a Trip", St. Paul Daily Globe Minnesota, 2 August 1889
[78] Hartford Currant, Hartford, Connecticut, 6 August 1889. Retrieved 15 April 2017
[79] "Edgefield has bloodied past", The Augusta Chronicles, Augusta, Georgia, 08 November 2003. http://chronicle.augusta.com/stories/2003/08/11/met_383852.shtml#.WPIlmdLyvct Accessed 15 April 2017
[80] "THE OFFICERS SUSPENDED", Pittsburgh Dispatch, Pittsburgh, PA., 6 August 1889. Retrieved 15 April 2017
[81] "A SCHEME THAT DIDN'T WORK", Pittsburgh Dispatch, Pittsburgh, PA., 10 August 1889. Retrieved 15 April 2017
[82] "THE JURY WITH FLEMON" Pittsburgh Dispatch, Pittsburgh. PA., 5 August 1889. Retrieved 15 April 2017

[83] "YELDELL IN COURT", Pittsburgh Dispatch, Pittsburgh, PA. 10 August 1889. Retrieved 15 April 2017
[84] Ibid.
[85] "YELDELL ACQUITTED", Pittsburgh Dispatch, 11 August 1889. Retrieved 15 April 2017
[86] Ibid.
[87] "YELDELL ACQUITTED", The Atlanta Constitution, Atlanta, GA. 11 August 1889. Retrieved 15 April 2017
[88] "YELDELL ACQUITTED", Pittsburgh Dispatch, 11 August 1889. Retrieved 15 April 2017
[89] Ibid.
[90] "Yeldell Acquitted", St. Louis Post-Dispatch, St. Louis, MO, 11 August 1889. Retrieved 15 April 2017
[91] "Rev. Flemon Acquitted.", The Pittsburgh Headlight, Pittsburgh, KA., 8 August 1889. Retrieved 15 April 2017
[92] "Morning Tribune", Altoona Tribune, Altoona PA., 13 August 1889. Retrieved 15 April 2017
[93] "A THRILLING ESCAPE", The Summit County Beacon, Akron, OH. 5 November 1890. Retrieved 15 April 2017
[94] ECI Centers – The Center for Civil Advocacy (CCA), http://www.tsulaw.edu/centers/ECI/centers/civil_advocacy.html accessed 29 March 2017
[95] The Sixth Floor Museum at Dealey Plaza, http://www.jfk.org/the-museum/ Accessed 29 March 2017
[96] The Sixth Floor Museum at Dealey Plaza, http://www.jfk.org/the-collections/oral-history/ Accessed 30 March 2017
[97] "Branches of the same tree: A family reunion for the history books", The Index Journal, Greenwood, SC 9 Sept 2016.

Made in the USA
Middletown, DE
27 March 2024